Economics for a Post-Material Future

Douglas E. Booth

Copyright © 2015 Douglas E. Booth
All rights reserved

Economics for a Post-Material Future
Published by Douglas E. Booth
Milwaukee, WI

ISBN-13: 978-1505857733
ISBN-10: 1505857732

Printed by CreateSpace

Table of Contents

Preface i
1 Introduction to Post-Material Philosophy 1
2 The Post-Material Turn 5
3 Millennials and the Post-Material Turn 15
4 Materialism and the Suburban Dream 21
5 The Turn to Downtown Living 31
6 Starving Artists and Their Existential Problem 42
7 Working Hours and the Creative Impulse 50
8 Philosophy Matters for Climate Change 58
9 The Experience Economy 75
10 Post-Material Philosophy 89
11 Macroeconomics for the Future 129
12 Economic Democracy 140
13 Our Post-Material Future 164
Bibliography 168
Index 179

Preface

When asked, most people could say something about their personal philosophy—those beliefs and values that guide them on their path through life. In their theorizing and empirical work, economists normally assume that we humans make choices in the world for the purpose of maximizing our well-being. The philosophies behind our choices rarely get much traction in economic research beyond the idea of maximization itself. This I believe to be mistaken. Beliefs and values indeed influence the choices we make, economic and otherwise. My contention in the pages ahead is that shifts in personal philosophies matter and can fundamentally alter economic arrangements and outcomes. We may seek to maximize our well being, but our notion of what this means shifts with time and circumstances. What's of importance to us today may not be so tomorrow.

To make my point in this book, I will describe a fundamental value shift underway globally and explore actual and potential economic changes flowing from it. This shift amounts to a weakening of an orientation to simple economic materialism and a strengthening of interest in more complex qualitative accomplishments and experiences that don't always require an expansion in private possessions. For economic materialists, the essential human purpose is the accumulation of material possessions even if basic biological survival is well assured. Economic materialists see the gaining of power, pleasure, status, social intercourse, creative accomplishment, and spirituality as heavily dependent on what one owns and privately consumes. Life is all about possessing and consuming, and little else. For post-materialists, access to material goods matters but is secondary to a life of meaning defined by a value-driven personal philosophy. The essential difference between materialism and post-materialism is one of emphasis. In the first case, the human psyche focuses on acquiring material possessions, and in the second it shifts to concern with not only the experiences of life but also the realization of an array of human values as the final source of meaning. In this shift we move further away from a basic quantitative and biological orientation to the satisfaction of physical needs and toward a qualitative satisfaction of wants for mental experiences. We in effect move from dwelling almost entirely on the material hardware of life to an expanded interest in its qualitative software.

Post-materialism is premised on already secure economic conditions and emphasizes the special importance in life of personal freedom and autonomy, social tolerance and informality, humane treatment of all individuals, protection of the natural environment, democratic participation in one's work and community life, and a self-creative approach to spiritual or philosophical connections beyond the self. Materialism by contrast presumes that life's meaning is best secured through material possessions. In practice of course, the two notions stand at the opposite ends of a spectrum of behavioral possibilities with most of us residing somewhere in between. In our modern daily experience materialism predominates and is intensely familiar to us. We in the affluent countries of the world today take for granted a materialistic consumerism that heavily influences our private and public life experience. Social scientists nonetheless point to an increase in post-materialist values among younger generations that are especially prevalent among those coming of age in conditions of reasonable economic security.

My purpose in the pages to follow is to review the evidence for a post-materialist value trend and to then establish and explain the economic changes flowing from it. My basic conclusion will be that personal philosophical outlooks have economic consequences. The future economy in a post-material world will feature such changes as these: more flexible working hours and shorter workweeks; a return to downtown living; an expanded clean energy sector and greenhouse gas emissions reductions; a substantial shift from acquisition of material possessions to more shared experiences and a rising demand for shared public goods; an activist fiscal policy to sustain employment in the face of weakening private sector consumption; and more expansive economic democracy and employee ownership. This vision looks like a political liberal's dream and a political conservative's worse nightmare. I could easily be wrong about its realization, but let me now tell you in the chapters to follow why I think I am right. Then you can judge.

1 Introduction to Post-Material Philosophy

The only personal philosophy worth thinking about is a "philosophy for the future." In the time given to us on this earth, how should we live and what should we do? This we have to decide. The future is all there is; the past is done and we can do nothing to change it; the present flits by as we stand around contemplating our fate. The past leaves an unavoidable deterministic legacy, but we aren't required to accept it in its entirety. We can't go back and change history and how it affects us, but we can alter our path as we move forward. Choosing what to do in life is our essential freedom, but just the possession of this option can be overpowering and leave us frozen in anxiety. Are we truly condemned to be free, as Jean-Paul Sartre tells us?[1] The idea of experiencing life, of having to decide how to live, as opposed to not existing at all, is both astonishing and deeply frightening. We can just trundle on and let the legacy of history and popular culture take us where it will; we can cave into the determinism of history and go with the flow. This is a choice. But we can also stand up and decide for ourselves what our future will be. Don't let your mistakes of the past overwhelm you; don't let the evil eye of others deter you from your chosen path. The future is your rose for the picking, but watch out for the thorns. Take lessons from history but don't let it rule your life. Strike out and take control.

These sentiments define the nature of the "existential" choice on how to lead our lives, one that inevitably involves us in a variety of either/or decisions, such as letting others choose for us instead of doing it ourselves, or seeking material wealth as opposed to goals that bring meaning to life but not necessarily as much money for buying things. In recent history most citizens of affluent, industrialized countries have chosen a materialist path, and most spend the better part of their waking hours getting a living and spending it. The undeniable wonders of modern material progress endow us with comfortable, pleasurable, healthy, and

---

[1]Jean-Paul Sartre, *Being and Nothingness* (New York: Washington Square Press, 1992).

interesting lives. Acquiring material possessions is fun, and in the process all of us together cause the economy tick along, creating employment and giving us all something to do.

While the immediate future will no doubt look much like the past, a slow but steady trend in human pursuits is taking us beyond a purely materialist existence. Even today not everyone follows strictly economic dreams. Some of us look outside of immediate possessive concerns to seek our meaning in life. Post-material pursuits take us beyond private hedonistic desires, such as the enjoying of a scoop of French vanilla ice cream, buying a new iPad, taking a cruise to the Caribbean, driving a Porsche, or wearing a brand new, fashionable pair of soccer shoes to practice. A post-materialist soccer player instead would want to advance the quality of game itself (as a soccer referee might), or the success of a particular team (as a cooperating team member would), and would not solely focus on obtaining personal glory or the opportunity to wear fancy soccer clothing or to drive a fancy car to the game. Post-materialist soccer would be valued for its own sake, not just for the immediate private pleasure the playing of it brings. In a similar vein, one can value for its own sake photographing beautiful landscapes, writing about philosophy, advocating for gun rights, seeking governmental limits on climate change, researching the causes of cancer, fixing and extending the life of an aging clothes dryer, putting a new roof on an older architecturally interesting house, creating a new microbrew, roasting a new variety of coffee, acting in a play by Oscar Wilde, or producing leafy green vegetables on Cairo, Egypt's rooftops to increase local family incomes, create green space in a city without much, and expand the supply of nutritional foods available to Cairenes.

To value post-materially is to possess a deep desire that some activity or being out in the world exists and flourishes into the future. True love is post-material and takes us outside strict self-concern, but pure lust is self-oriented and focuses on satisfying pleasurable desires. There is nothing wrong with lust and pleasure, but we humans also express passionate attachments to activities and beings outside of our personal skins. Only in a state of non-possessive, other-orientation do we forget our ego and experience the wonders of the world as they stand for themselves. We can experience beings and objects as something over which we desire power and control, or we can appreciate them transcendently as free and independent with a physical path of their own in time and space and a virtual one in human thought and sensibilities. We can enjoy the continued existence of an ancient and beautiful musical instrument, such as a Stradivarius violin or a Guarneri cello, and the continued presence and performance of beautiful music that can be understood only in the human mind, and we can do this without personal possession or control. The same is the case for colorful wildflower-laden subalpine meadows, world series baseball games, great works of philosophy, well tended gardens, Shakespearian plays, French impressionist paintings, the architectural wonders of Barcelona, the military precision of troops in formation led by the tunes of a marching band, jazz performances in the bars of New Orleans, or a stable climate free of greenhouse gas perils.

For post-materialists, experiences stand above consumer possessions in importance. Possessions are necessary to life, but it's experiences that count for life's greatest satisfactions. Post-materialism takes us beyond our strictly personal interests toward a more open and less self-conscious connection with the larger world. We will always worry about our own, private well-being, but our new-found post-materialist values can move us to look outward beyond our personal skin toward the amazements of existence as such. The idea of experiencing life, as opposed to not existing at all, is both astonishing and deeply frightening as already noted, but can foster in us a sense of wonder and cause us to engage in care for all that we love, and, in particular for the earth itself, the source of our being.

All this sounds great, even utopian, as an offering of a better future for anyone disenchanted with modern life, but I am getting ahead of myself. Post-materialism as a trend has only just begun with barely perceptible baby-steps. None of us will become full-fledged post-materialists overnight. We need to understand the importance of our materialist ways first, and then we can look into the meaning and nature of slowly rising and not much noticed post-materialist practices in the midst of our material affluence. What we will see in this exercise is that philosophy truly matters. If our philosophical values slowly but inexorably change over time, the way we live, and the impact we have on the world around us, will also change. By looking at trends in the values we possess, we can gain insights into the direction we are headed.

2 The Post-Material Turn

The Google founders, Sergey Brin and Larry Page, started out to create the best Internet search engine there is, not to make a ton of money. It took a while for them to accept the idea of ads related to searches as the path to generating revenue. The usual web ads that obnoxiously flash at you or fill up your screen Brin hated. Brin and Page instead happened on the brilliant idea of simple, unobtrusive text ads that turned out to be a gold mine. Simplicity, speed, and efficiency are what Brin and Page were after, not the money. They didn't like the usual hierarchic modes of business organization and chose a flatter more decentralized and chaotic form for Google, but it worked. Informal meetings and intense, competitive recreation along with free food kept the place running. Brin didn't like marketing and wanted to use the marketing budget at one point to inoculate Chechen refugees against cholera because it would be a good thing to do and could bring attention to Google. Google's well-known guiding moral standard is "don't be evil." On the job physical activity energizes life at Google—pool, ping pong, and, of course, roller hockey, the one most encouraged by Brin and Page. The original workspaces were filled with crash cots, funky second hand furniture, makeshift room dividers, exercise balls, and ever-present white boards for scribbling down the next big ideas. The annual ski trips for Googlers (i.e. Google employees) were legendary for their decompressing party atmosphere. Google is an offbeat place to work like no other, but to become a Googler means working long hours with others in small groups, accepting meritocratic values, and being assertive, creative, a risk taker, and playful. Constant anxiety about measuring up comes with the Googler territory.[1]

In the world of high tech, it's not your ethnic origin and social background that matters. It's the software code you have written lately or the successful new application or popular new gadget you have helped to create that confers status. Young techies are a tolerant lot; they judge according to merit and accomplishment, not

---

[1]Douglas Edwards, *I'm Feeling Lucky: The Confessions of Google Employee Number 59* (New York: Houghton Mifflin, 2011).

according to appearance or skin color, and they delight in a wide range of behavior patterns and personal styles. Tattoos and body piercing jewelry are fine as well as unusual tastes in music, art, or sexual practices. The experience of life matters, not where one comes from or what one owns.

The high tech world, despite its incredible financial success, embodies a modest beginning of a movement away from purely materialist concerns toward post-materialistic personal self-expression, social tolerance, and interesting life experiences. Seeking meaning in life boils down to adopting and pursuing purposes about which one cares passionately. If we have strong materialist inclinations, then we will find meaning predominantly in the economic arena where we will pursue wealth and material possessions. If we follow a post-materialist path, our actions in the world will take us beyond strictly economic pursuits. If you did nothing but look to advertising and the popular media, you might think that post-materialism is a utopian dream, but social scientists over the past several decades have detected a modest but persistent shift favoring values that take us beyond a predominant desire for wealth and consumption.

I don't want to force you through a tedious, article-by-article, academic-style summary of the research to prove that post-materialism is indeed a significant trend that will take us into a new and different future, but I do want to give you a flavor of what the post-materialist idea is all about. What I am going summarize for you now is not philosophical speculation, but actual, real world research findings on human attitudes and belief. Before I do this, I want to acknowledge the one researcher responsible more than any other for discovering the post-materialist trend, University of Michigan professor, Ronald Inglehart, whose findings in the 1970s set off a wave of academic research that continues to this day. So, let's get started with our post-material philosophy for the future.[2]

Post-materialism is measured from data obtained through surveys that ask about respondent social priorities. Suppose you attach high priorities to such social goals as (1) protecting freedom of speech, (2) giving people more say in important government

---

[2]Ronald F. Inglehart and Paul R. Abramson, "Economic Security and Value Change," *American Political Science Review* 88(1994).

decisions, (3) seeing that people have more say about how things are done at their jobs and in their communities, (4) trying to make our cities and countryside more beautiful, (5) progress toward a less impersonal and more humane society, and (6) progress toward a society in which ideas count more than money. Then you are a post-materialist. Suppose instead you attach high priorities to such goals as (7) maintaining order in the nation, (8) fighting rising prices, (9) a high level of economic growth, (10) making sure this country has strong defense forces, (11) a stable economy, and (12) the fight against crime. In this case you are a materialist. If your priorities are mixed you lay on a spectrum between. If your highest priorities are all materialist, that's what you are; if you highest priorities all go the other direction your are a post-materialist; if you have a mix of highest choice priorities you are neither.

Early research on post-materialism used just two post-materialist priorities: (1) protecting freedom of speech and (2) giving people more say in important government decisions, and two materialist priorities: (7) maintaining order in the nation, and (8) fighting rising prices. Survey respondents were asked to choose their highest priority for options (1) and (7) and again for options (2) and (8). Post-materialists were counted as those choosing (1) and (2) for their highest priorities, materialists as choosing (7) and (8), and the rest as mixed. Later, a more complex set of questions using all twelve items became the research standard for developing a more refined index for measuring post-materialism.[3] Nonetheless, statistical research has confirmed that the simpler 4-question approach performs almost as well as do the 12-questions in measuring post-materialism.[4]

If you are in your twenties, you are more likely to be a post-materialist than if you are in your seventies. If you are young, you probably grew up in a period of economic prosperity, and if you are older you most likely faced economic deprivations in your pre-adult years. In general, younger generations today in Europe,

---

[3]For example, see Chum-chih Chang and Te-Sheng Chen, "Idealism versus Reality: Empirical Test of Postmaterialism in China and Taiwan," *Issues and Studies* 49, no. 2 (2013).
[4]Paul R. Abramson and Ronald F. Inglehart, *Value Change in Global Perspective* (Ann Arbor: University of Michigan Press, 1995); Inglehart and Abramson, "Economic Security and Value Change."

America, and the prosperous Asian countries experienced secure economic conditions in their youth while older generations suffered material challenges when they were growing up. Because our basic values are formed by the time we reach adulthood, whether or not we face economic scarcity or social upheavals in our youth matters. As we age, our value orientations fluctuate to some extent with economic conditions, but our basic outlook doesn't change much. Those with materialist leanings in their youth keep them for life just as post-materialists retain their basic values. If we look at a cross-section of society today, younger birth cohorts tend to be more post-materialist than older, and, as time passes and younger replace older cohorts, the ratio of post-materialists to materialists increases in affluent, industrialized countries. In the early 1970s, materialists heavily outnumbered post-materialists in Western Europe, but by 2006 post-materialists slightly outnumbered materialists, and by this time in the U.S. post-materialists outnumber materialists by a ratio of 2 to 1. The most post-materialist country of all, Sweden, possesses a 5 to 1 ratio for post-materialists to materialists.[5]

Beginning recently in the 21st Century, younger birth cohorts in European countries became slightly less post-materialist than their immediate predecessor generations, probably because economic crisis and stagnation reduced economic prospects for new job market entrants. Among the youngest adult generation in the U.S., post-materialism is under threat as well because of rising unemployment.[6] Nonetheless, the post-material turn in affluent countries still looks to have plenty of life left in it despite recent economic setbacks. The U.S. economy is on the mend and economic optimism for the future is greatest among the youngest adults. Once Europeans get over their love affair with economic austerity and engage in expansionary government spending similar to the U.S., economic opportunities for younger generations will improve and they will likely recover from any angst about their material future and return to the post-materialist fold.

---

[5]Ronald F. Inglehart, "Changing Values among Western Publics from 1970 to 2006," *West European Politics* 31, no. 1-2 (2008).
[6]See the next chapter on Millennials.

The brightest prospects for growth in post-material values lies in those countries that have yet to experience economic success. On the global stage, post-materialism bears a strong relationship to per capita incomes, as one would expect. Countries with high poverty rates and modest incomes today have a strong materialist orientation, but as incomes increase across countries, the incidence of post-materialist values rises dramatically.[7] As countries develop and create conditions of economic security and political stability for their younger generations, the incidence of post-material values expands, even where affluence is new and novel. In China, for instance, post-materialist values have arisen amongst an emergent middle class and surprisingly look to be relatively more prevalent than in more affluent and democratic Taiwan.[8]

A shift to a post-material philosophy matters for everyday life. Post-materialism leads to a more outward social orientation and substantially enlarged demands for political expression, a result of much importance around the world. Countries with a high incidence of post-materialism tend be strongly democratic, possess a high degree of tolerance toward homosexuality, promote gender equity, and rank high in interpersonal trust.[9] For post-materialists, free self-expression is a big deal. Post-materialists also give significant political support to public actions that expands environmental protection or otherwise improves the quality of life. The Green Party in Europe garners much of its backing from citizens with post-materialist leanings.[10] Post-materialists are less supportive of older social issues involving unions and working class advancement, and don't always place themselves on a liberal-conservative political spectrum. The rise of the "independent voter" and post-materialism coincide, to which politicians increasingly need to pay attention in order to win elections. This

---

[7]Ibid.; Inglehart and Abramson, "Economic Security and Value Change."
[8]Chang and Chen, "Idealism versus Reality: Empirical Test of Postmaterialism in China and Taiwan."
[9]Inglehart, "Changing Values among Western Publics from 1970 to 2006."; Inglehart and Abramson, "Economic Security and Value Change."; Christian Welzel and Ronald F. Inglehart, "The Role of Ordinary People in Democratization," *Journal of Democracy* 19(2008).
[10]Ronald F. Inglehart, "Public Support for Environmental Protection: Objective Problems and Subjective Values in 43 Societies," *Political Science and Politics* 28(1995).

means giving less truck to class issues and more to advancing social tolerance and the quality of life for all.[11]

We all possess a wider range of value orientations than those covered by post-materialist research, an essential conclusion of well-regarded survey studies by Israeli social psychologist, Shalom H. Schwartz, on what he calls "basics human values." These include "power, achievement, hedonism, stimulation, self-direction, universalism, benevolence, tradition, conformity, and security." Universalism for Schwartz means "understanding, appreciation, tolerance, and protection for the welfare of all people and for nature," and benevolence refers to the "preservation and enhancement of welfare of people with whom one is in frequent contact." The other basic values have their expected, ordinary language meanings in Schwartz's work.[12] Although post-materialism encompasses a comparatively narrow range of social goals, it nonetheless correlates positively with the broader "basic human values" of "universalism" and "self-direction," and negatively with commitments to "tradition," "social conformity," and personal "security." In other words, many post-materialists express special concern about both the welfare of all human beings and the natural world and put a high value personal autonomy, but don't like the straight jackets of too much safety and obedience to social norms. Post-materialists also commonly lack strong attachment to self-enhancement values, such as "power" and "achievement." In short, post-materialists possess a broad "other orientation" in their personal outlook as opposed to materialists who express their strongest commitments inwardly to achievement, security, and social conformity.[13] We will see later that the

---

[11] Inglehart, "Changing Values among Western Publics from 1970 to 2006."; Inglehart and Abramson, "Economic Security and Value Change."

[12] Shalom H. Schwartz, "Are There Universal Aspects in the Structure and Contents of Human Values?," *Journal of Social Issues* 50, no. 4 (1994).

[13] Tilo Beckers, Pascal Siegers, and Anabel Kuntz, "Congruence and Performance of Value Concepts in Social Research," *Survey Research Methods* 6(2012). Schwartz and other researchers construct human values indices by asking survey respondents to rank specific values as guiding principle in their lives on a 1-9 importance scale. A universalism index, for instance, is created by averaging scores for the specific values of equality, social justice, environmental protection, unity with nature, inner harmony, a world at peace, a world of beauty, wisdom, and broad mindedness. Universalism, and other basic value indices, can in turn be correlated with a post-materialism index obtained from the same sample to test for statistical significance.

connection between post-materialism and a universal outlook has a particular importance, especially since it runs against the grain of a strong and exclusive human attachment to strictly local and personally known human communities and natural landscapes.

Given their suspicion of orthodoxy and tradition, post-materialists don't warm easily to conventional religious practice, but this doesn't mean they lack spiritual inclinations. In Europe, where the trend to post-materialist values is especially strong, traditional religion is experiencing a sharp decline in popularity.[14] Taking its place appears to be an alternative spirituality that picks and chooses from a range of notions about the sacred. Instead of buying into pre-digested religious doctrines and subordinating the self to allegedly transcendent truths about the nature of being, spiritual practitioners increasingly rely on their own creativity to develop their patterns of belief. For a time, the so-called "New Age" movement, rooted in such phenomenon as astrology, reincarnation, fortune telling, and contact with the dead, gained sway as a replacement for traditional religion, but such beliefs are now on the wane. Instead, spiritual practices have become more amorphous and pragmatic with a heavy orientation to improving one's subjective experience of life where a connection to whatever is seen as a sacred is what really matters.

This new kind of spiritual phenomenon is variously referred to as post-Christian spirituality, or private or alternative religiosity, but it all is essentially the same phenomenon—a turn to spiritual beliefs and practices unaffiliated with any organized religion. Those who profess and practice an unaffiliated spirituality commonly hold post-materialist beliefs, including such untraditional views as support for gender equity, tolerance of a wide range of sexual behaviors, and the practice of non-hierarchical relationships within the family between parent and child. The spiritually unaffiliated often practice meditation and seek for a deeper and unconventional meaning of life free of existing doctrine, be it Christian or New Age. By contrast, religious traditionalists typically believe in a personal god, attend

---

[14]Dick Houtman and Stef Aupers, "The Spiritual Turn and the Decline of Tradition: The Spread of Post-Christian Spirituality in 14 Western Countries, 1981–2000," *Journal for the Scientific Study of Religion* 46(2007).

church, and belong to religious organizations, and New Agers, as just noted, claim belief in astrology, reincarnation, fortune telling, or contact with the dead.[15] Spiritual individualists are more prone to post-materialist opinions about social priorities, express greater support for environmental protection, and have a higher level of educational achievement than either New Agers or religious traditionalists.[16] One might think that post-materialists would be inclined to New-Age views, but New Agers surprisingly have a conservative outlook on materialism akin to what one might expect of a low-income, religious fundamentalism common in the U.S.

Let's take a moment to summarize post-materialism's content. Above all else, post-materialists value the right to self-expression in the lives of everyone and possess a high degree of social and cultural tolerance. Post-materialism itself is defined narrowly, but adherents oftentimes express other values that reflect an outward orientation to the world at large. The great modern challenge is finding common ground amongst a huge array of private interests and tribe-like attachments. Universalist values, which profess a concern for the welfare of humanity as a whole and for all of nature's beings, ease this challenge, and, fortuitously, post-materialists are often "universalists." Even though they lack an interest in conventional religion, post-materialists are not a bunch of atheists, but instead tend towards spirituality of an unorthodox kind. The big differences between liberal post-materialists and conservative materialists come in their respective attitudes towards society's institutions. While both post-materialists and conservatives subscribe to freedom of expression and the elimination of political oppression, conservatives express stronger attachments than liberals to hierarchies and authority, group loyalty, traditional religions and values, and limits on the role of the state in the economy and society. Liberal post-materialists to the contrary are skeptical of authority, hierarchy, and organized groups of any kind, avoid organized religion, and often take an untraditional path through life. While post-materialists sometimes express libertarian attitudes towards government, many take a

---

[15]Magnus Hagevi, "Beyond Church and State: Private Religiosity and Post-Materialist Political Opinion among Individuals in Sweden," *Journal of Church and State* 54(2012).
[16]Pal Ketil Botvar, "Alternative Religion – A New Political Cleavage?: An Analysis of Norwegian Survey Data on New Forms of Spirituality," *Politics and Religion* 2(2009).

pragmatic position about the necessity of government for providing essential public goods, restraining the excesses of a free market economy, and limiting religious oppression.[17]

Yet another way researchers look at shifting philosophical outlooks is to employ questions from the World Values Survey to measure orientations on a spectrum between survival at the low end of a scale and self-expression at the high end. The resulting self-expression scale is constructed from responses to questions about one's (1) post-materialist orientation, (2) degree of happiness, (4) willingness to sign a political petition, (5) presence of a positive (as opposed to a negative) attitude toward homosexuality, and (6) level of trustfulness of others. A positive (high scaled) response to these items indicates a self-expressive orientation, while the opposite (low scaled) infers a survival orientation. Those who worry about survival are materialists, unhappy with their lives, unwilling to participate in politics, lack tolerance for homosexuality, and don't trust others, and self-expressers hold the opposite attitudes. The self-expression measure includes post-materialism, but goes beyond it. Studies using the World Values Survey confirm self-expresser support for gender equity, autonomy in the workplace, political freedom, and environmental protection, all of which comply with a "universalist" outlook for personal values. In survey research, the World Values Survey is a big deal because it covers so many countries with comparatively large population samples for each.[18]

Philosophical values documented in the World Values Survey turn out to not only fall on survival-self-expression continuum, but spread out along a traditional-secular/rational spectrum as well. Traditionalists see (1) belief in God as important in their lives, (2) think children should be taught religious faith and obedience as opposed to independence and self-expression, (3) see pride in nationality as important, (4) have substantial respect for authority, and (5) oppose abortion. Rational secularists express the opposite values. Countries with strongly traditionalist values tend to score low on the survival-self-expression scale, but many of these,

---

[17]Jonathan Haidt, *The Righteous Mind: Why Good People are Divided by Politics and Religion* (New York: Random House, 2012).
[18]Ronald F. Inglehart and Wayne E. Baker, "Modernization, Cultural Change, and the Persistence of Traditional Values," *American Sociological Review* 65(2000).

nonetheless exhibit a modest but steady trend to a self-expressive, post-materialist outlook over time. Specific religions score at different levels on the traditional-secular/rational scale, with Protestants tending to score high toward the secular end of the scale, Muslims low toward the traditional end, and Catholics in the middle.[19] Religion matters, but religious orientation does nothing to reverse the trend over time toward more prevalent self-expression values as more youthful post-materialist birth cohorts expand their population share, even for a highly traditionalist society such as Egypt.[20]

None of this means that deeply Muslim countries will become bastions of liberal democracy and personal freedom anytime soon, but, simply, that there exists an underlying modest but inexorable movement of values in a more post-material, self-expressive, universalist direction. Nor is it likely that the red-blue state division in the U.S. will disappear quickly. The trend to post-materialism by its nature moves at a modest pace, especially in the U.S. and Europe where a strong contrary trend of population aging dampens political and cultural liberalization. The future will be post-material, but it won't arrive overnight.

---

[19]Ronald F. Inglehart, "The Worldviews of Islamic Publics in Global Perspective," in *Values and Perceptions of the Islamic and Middle Eastern Publics*, ed. Mansoor Moaddel (New York: Palgrave, 2007).
[20] Randall Kuhn, "On the Role of Human Development in the Arab Spring," (Boulder: Institute of Behaviorial Science, University of Colorado, 2011).

3 Millennials and the Post-Material Turn

The Great Recession of 2007-2009 amounted to the most serious global economic reversal since the Great Depression of the 1930s. Add to this 9-11 and its economic disruptions and the subsequent wars in Iraq and Afghanistan, the first decade of the new century turned out to be an unsettling time to come of age for Millennials, the latest generational cohort to enter into adulthood. The older members of this group came of age in the prosperous and tranquil 1990s, but circumstances have darkened for younger members. It's too soon to tell for sure whether early 21st Century economic and social disruption will foster a return to a more materialist outlook by Millennials compared to their immediate predecessor generations, but we can look to some initial survey data to see if a materialist turn is in the cards for the future.

The "Millennial" generation includes those individuals born between 1981 and 1997 that currently ranges in age from 18 to 34. Their predecessors for attitudinal comparison are Generation X whose birth years range from 1965 through 1980, Baby Boomers born from 1946 to 1964, and the Silent Generation birthed between 1928 and 1945. The division of the living population into specific generations by age assumes that each possesses unique cultural attributes related to their particular historical experience. Post-materialist research hypothesizes that economic and social conditions prevailing as we grow up deeply shapes our fundamental outlook for life.[1] As one generation replaces another over the long haul, the predominance of particular social and political values in the population as a whole will change in accordance with divergent generational experiences. The Silent Generation, for instance, came of age in a globally tumultuous era of economic depression and global warfare, and by comparison Baby Boomer's grew up in relative economic tranquility, although they were exposed to the stresses of the Cold War and the social and political disruptions of the 1960s. By comparison, Generation X came of age in the socially placid and relatively prosperous

---

[1]Inglehart and Abramson, "Economic Security and Value Change."

1970s and 1980s. In the popular press certain stereotypes of generational outlooks gain currency and become topics of daily conversation. Millennials, for example, get accused of being self-centered and possessing excessive expectations for rapid economic advancement in comparison to their Generation X and Baby Boom predecessors, although, as we will now see, the reality, according to survey research, is more nuanced. The question I want to address here is whether the Millennials continue the historical trend toward post-materialist values or take a U-turn back to materialism. Because Millennials have entered adulthood only since the turn of the century, research on their beliefs and values is just beginning, and any findings so far are necessarily preliminary.

According to a 2014 Pew research survey, Millennials differ from older generations in the following ways: (1) a lower percent are married currently than past generations at the same age; (2) a bigger proportion is less trusting of others; (3) those who have jobs are more upbeat about their financial future than their older colleagues; (4) in the last presidential election 60% of 18-29 years old voters cast their ballot for Obama while just 44% of 65+ years old voters did the same; (5) a greater percent claim to have liberal political values; (6) a lower percent say they believe in God or see themselves as religious; (7) a larger percent claim to be supporters of gay rights, interracial marriage, marijuana legalization, and an expanded role for government, but a smaller percent see themselves as environmentalists or as a patriotic persons; and (8) a larger percent possess, or are tolerant of, tattoos and body jewelry.[2] Above all, Millennials tell us in this survey that they possess a high degree of tolerance for others and strongly support personal self-expression. They also have a relatively liberal political outlook and aren't rushing into the fold of traditional religion or patriotic commitment. In all these values, they look to continue the post-material trend. The exceptions include a lesser concern for environmental issues and a lessening in trust of others relative to older generations, contrary to the usual post-materialist norms.

Given their alleged self-focus, Millennials surprisingly subscribe to "family values" at levels equal to their older peers in a

---

[2]Pew Research Center, "Millennials in Adulthood: Detached from Institutions, Networked with Friends," (2014).

2009 Pew survey.[3] Millennials claim that "being a good parent" is one of the most important things in their lives to the tune of 52 percent, not far off the 50 percent figure for those over thirty. This is substantially above the 15 percent of Millennials claiming that "being successful in a high paying career" is one of the most important things in their lives, although the over thirty respondents comes in at a lower 7 percent on this survey option. Both those under and over 30 have similar numbers for "helping others in need" at 21 and 20 percent respectively. From these numbers one is hard pressed to see much narcissism in Millennials. It is true that Millennials aren't supporting "family values" by getting married as quickly as older generations did, but diminished economic prospects brought to us by the Great Recession offer the best explanation for this tardiness.

Surveys of American high school students and entering college freshmen paint a picture of Millennials more in tune with their popular conception as a strongly self-oriented generation.[4] Compared to Baby Boomers at the same age, Millennials attached more importance to extrinsic goals such as money, image, and fame than intrinsically valued purposes such as self-acceptance, affiliation, and community. Between Generation X and the Millennials, trust in others, interest in social problems, and willingness to do something for the environment all declined, though participation in community service rose. In these attitudes we find support for the idea that Millennials can be referred to as generation "Me" as oppose to "We."

The same percent (74%) of Millennials in the American Freshman survey see "being very well off financially" and "raising a family" as important life goals, placing key forms of self- and other-oriented behavior at equal magnitudes. This is in marked contrast to the 2014 Pew survey of Millennials as a whole where "being a good parent" ranks much higher as an important goal (60%) than "having a successful career" (15%), putting other-oriented behavior on a higher plane than self-concern. This raises the possibility that values reported by high school seniors or

---

[3]Pew Research Center, "Millenials: Confident, Connected, Open to Change," (2010).
[4]Jean M. Twenge, W. Keith Campbell, and Elise C. Freeman, "Generational Differences in Young Adults' Life Goals, Concern for Others, and Civic Orientation, 1966-2009," *Journal of Personality and Social Psychology* 102, no. 5 (2012).

college freshman may not be cast in stone. Economic success seems to have been downgraded in the Pew 2014 survey by older Millennials relative to their high school senior and college freshmen leanings. In practice there looks to be more "We" to generation "Me" than suggested by surveys of high school seniors and college freshmen alone.

The diminished support by Millennials for environmentalism remains a mystery given their other post-material tendencies. Global surveys through 2009 find post-materialism to be a statistically significant factor in explaining environmental concern the world over.[5] To the contrary for the U.S., a recent study[6] finds environmental concern to depend positively on age, not negatively as one would expect if post-materialism, a youth-oriented phenomena, mattered significantly for environmental concern. Although being young fails to positively affects environmental concern, liberal political leanings and a pro-environmental philosophy do, attitudes generally expressed by post-materialist Millennials. Limited support by Millennials for the environment may emanate from their lack of trust in others. Researchers find that trust is a positive determinant of support for environmental protection,[7] but Millennials possess lower average trust levels than older generations.[8] Why this is the case remains unexplained. Perhaps lower than average Millennial trust arises from the recent sharp decline in the U.S. economy, and attendant darkened economic prospects for young job market entrants, brought on in large measure by their elders' financial speculations and over-borrowing. Similarly, Millennials might also worry that fossil-fuel influenced politicians, pandering to campaign contributing, moneyed interests, can't be trusted to actually do anything about the environment. Given this truth, why bother much about the

---

[5]Lee Ahern, "The Role of Media System Development in the Emergence of Postmaterialist Values and Environmental Concern: A Cross-National Analysis," *Social Science Quarterly* 93, no. 2 (2012).
[6]Xinsheng Liu, Arnold Vedlitz, and Liu Shi, "Examing the Determinants of Public Environmental Concern, Evidence from National Public Surveys," *Environmental Science and Policty* 39(2014).
[7]E. Tjernstrom and T. Tietenberg, "Do Differences in Attitudes Explain Differences in National Climate Change Policies?," *Ecological Economics* 65(2012).
[8]Pew Research Center, "Millennials in Adulthood: Detached from Institutions, Networked with Friends," (2014).

issue? On top of the trust problem, declining incomes earned by Millennials, due to economic disruption, and mushrooming Millennial educational debt could together be reducing a willingness to spend hard earned incomes on higher taxes or energy costs for environmental protection. On the other hand, the liberal political leanings of Millennials should be pulling their environmental concern upward. Sorting out these conflicting forces in explaining Millennial environmental attitudes is a statistical exercise yet to be performed.

In sum, Millennials in the U.S. express post-material and liberal values but environmentalism is not currently as high on their agenda as it is for others. The issues that most concern Millennials instead are free self-expression and social tolerance. Millennials claim to be politically independent, but in practice a substantial majority voted for a Democrat, Barack Obama, in the last two elections, and, like Democrats, they support a strong social safety net and favor government action to achieve it. At work they desire to be kept in the loop on larger organizational strategies, want regular feedback on how they are doing, and express impatience for advancement. They prefer working in groups and controlling their own schedule. As already noted, surveys offer mixed signals on their expectations for material gain. Research on high school seniors and college freshman point to a special Millennial desire for fame and fortune, but other surveys suggest they differ only modestly from their generational predecessors in this regard.[9] Millennials (like post-materialists generally) have detached themselves from traditional religious practices, avoiding church membership and attendance. Their political and spiritual independence gives them a reputation for disinterest in traditional community connections. They socialize at a distance through digital media more than anyone else, and they prefer informal group attachments. Although not joiners, they do more volunteer work than their elders. Cultural informality and idiosyncrasy seems to be their hallmark, to the consternation of those committed to such traditional values as respect for authority and loyalty to church and country. Millennials in the U.S. express strong support

---

[9]Twenge, Campbell, and Freeman, "Generational Differences in Young Adults' Life Goals, Concern for Others, and Civic Orientation, 1966-2009."

for the usual post-materialist values, except for environmentalism and trust in others. Millennials will likely continue the advancement of the post-materialist trend in the U.S., but probably at a pace dampened by recent economic upheavals. Time and the next World Values Survey will tell. For now, the most we can say with any confidence is that the Millennial generation may be dampening the post-material turn by younger generations, but not bringing it to a halt.[10]

I think what post-material Millennials are telling us is this: Get off your materialist economic treadmill, smell the roses, and look outward to the experience and adventure of life in the world outside your skin. Unfortunately, our economy, and its prospects for full employment, now relies on a materialist inclination, namely our tendency to expand ownership of material possessions, but this can be fixed with changes in our current economic arrangements. Before we dig into the reality and needs of a post-material future, let's make sure we have a clear picture of the wonders economic materialism has brought us historically. Then we will be in a good position to tackle how post-materialism is already changing the way we live, and to describe the economic reforms that will take us to a successful post-material future.

---

[10]Center, "Millenials: Confident, Connected, Open to Change."; Center, "Millennials in Adulthood: Detached from Institutions, Networked with Friends."

4 Materialism and the Suburban Dream

Since economic materialism remains the dominant form of modern life, we need to insure that we have a solid understanding of its nature and continuing importance. This we will accomplish with a quick run-through of an essential 20th Century manifestation of economic materialism, the rise of suburban living. To repeat, doing this will give us the background we need to put in sharp relief the nature and importance of the post-material turn.

***

The quest by philosophers for a singular and final explanation of the meaning of life has been largely given up as a fruitless exercise. Instead, we are left to deal with this task on our own. Most of us say that we believe in God, and that religion takes care of all questions of ultimate meaning. The trouble with this kind of response for us Americans is that we pay lip service to religion, but then what we really do is go to the mall. We are materialists, body and soul, through and through, and we live accordingly. We find our meaning not in the heavens, but in goods. As materialists we believe that the essential purpose in life is to gain access to financial resources and to use them to acquire material possessions. Accomplishing this purpose is our passion. Our temples are the Mall of America and Amazon.com. Meaning comes from adopting purposes and values about which we care passionately and pursuing them through actions in the world, and the predominant form of meaning today is deeply materialist.

Our dream of where to live for over a century in this country has been fundamentally suburban; the city doesn't suit our consumerist ways as well and conveniently as the suburbs. Fifth Avenue in New York and the Magnificent Mile in Chicago have consumer palaces we love to visit, but most of us can't afford to buy much in these places. Our real consumer paradise is in the suburban malls and big box stores where we can find an abundance of treasures we can actually afford, and where we can drive right up and walk right in to buy what our heart desires. We can't afford the big city cathedrals of luxury retailing for the elite, but we are blessed with the affordable and accessible big box suburban churches of consumption for the middle class, and, of course,

Amazon where today with a touch of our finger on a keyboard can buy us our dreams.

You might think I am out to ridicule the vast majority of Americans who enjoy the delights of accumulating consumer possessions, but this would not be too smart given the current predominance of materialist sentiments. Instead, I will begin by reinforcing the significance and importance of the suburban consumption machine and those who drive it. By-and-large, despite what many academics say, suburban dwellers are happy people, and they want to stay that way. For good reason they choose the suburbs—the one place where they can most fully realize their material dreams. Most importantly, these are the people who keep the economy humming, and when they face unemployment, declining housing values, and foreclosures, material life suffers for nearly everyone. Lets take a quick look at what survey researchers have found out about materialism and life satisfaction.

**

Many happiness researchers postulate that materialists will be less satisfied than others because they are caught up on an economic treadmill that requires more and more of the day earning and buying in order to sustain the delights of consumption. Life on this treadmill sacrifices a deeper happiness that comes from having the time to engage fully in a variety of satisfying pursuits: interacting with family and friends; involvement in community activities, such as amateur sports, charitable causes, politics, or church; putting energy into some activity so engaging as to cause one to lose all sense of self-consciousness; or accomplishing some purpose that expresses one's deepest commitment to highly regarded personal values.[1] The losing of self-consciousness through intense engagement psychologists refer to as flow, and a wide variety of activities can produce it—pitching in a highly competitive baseball game, writing important software code,

---

[1] Garhammer, Manfred. "Pace and Enjoyment of Life." *Journal of Happiness Studies* 3 (2002): 217-56; Ed Diener, Richard E. Lucas, and Christie Napa Scollon, "Beyond the Hedonic Treadmill: Revising the Adaptation Theory of Well-Being," *Social Indicators Research* 37(2009); Ed Diener and Robert Biswas-Diener, "Will Money Increase Subjective Well-Being?: A Literature Review and Guide to Needed Research," *Social Indicators Research* 37(2009).

working on a painting of a desert landscape at sunset, pursuing a deer with a bow and arrow, or climbing a fourteener, such as San Luis Peak in Colorado. The same is true of accomplishing a valued purpose such as writing a book about how to bring climate change to a halt, successfully helping elect a candidate for political office who will support cap and trade, or completing a lay sermon about belief in God before a Unitarian church congregation.[2]

Survey research has indeed confirmed that materialists do experience less life satisfaction than others, primarily because they spend less time with their families and more on economic pursuits.[3] But recent findings paint a more nuanced picture of the relationship between materialism and happiness. In college, more materialistic students tend to be more outgoing and popular, less accomplished academically, and more likely to take up majors with the best income earning prospects, such as business and engineering, than their less materialistic counterparts. After college, many, but not all, materialistically oriented graduates achieve financial success. Those that do turn out to be just as satisfied with their lives as their peers who care less about making money, but those who aspire to financial accomplishment and fail to achieve it experience a small but statistically significantly lower level of life satisfaction than others, again because of less time spent with family. Actual economic success in effect compensates for lost satisfaction from extra time on an economic treadmill, but if you jump on the treadmill and fail to advance, your happiness suffers. In sum, materialistic suburbanites who achieve economic success appear to be as happy as anyone else, and those who fail suffer for it, but not by much.[4]

***

---

[2]M. Joseph Sirgy and Jiyun Wu, "The Pleasant Life, the Engaged Life, and the Meaningful Life: What about the Balanced Life?," Journal of Happiness Studies 10, no. 2 (2007).
[3]Diener and Biswas-Diener, "Will Money Increase Subjective Well-Being?: A Literature Review and Guide to Needed Research."
[4]Carol Nickerson, Norbert Schwarz, and Ed Diener, "Financial aspirations, financial success, and overall life satisfaction: who? and how?," *Journal of Happiness Studies* 8, no. 4 (2007); Carol Nickerson et al., "Zeroing in on the dark side of the American dream: A Closer Look at the Negative Consequences of the Goal for Financial Success," *Psychological Science* 14(2003).

An entertaining writer skilled at explaining how we extract meaning from materialism is James Twitchell. Consider the quote that begins the final chapter of his book, *Lead Us Into Temptation: The Triumph of American Materialism*.[5] Here it is:

> Sell them their dreams. Sell them what they longed for and hoped for and almost despaired of having. Sell them hats by splashing sunlight across them. Sell them dreams—dreams of country clubs and proms and visions of what might happen if only. After all, people don't buy things to have things. They buy things to work for them. They buy hope—hope of what your merchandise will do for them. Sell them this hope and you won't have to worry about selling them goods.

These are the words of Helen Landon Cass, a female radio announcer, spoken before a convention of salesman in 1923. Is American materialism indeed the answer to the quest for meaning in life? Cass seems to think so and so does Twitchell. Anyone concerned with economics and the pursuit of meaning can't ignore what Cass and Twitchell have to say given the extraordinary role of consumer desire in our global economic reality today. How could acquiring possessions be an act of self-creation that defines what we care about in the world? What exactly is the power of stuff? Let's see what Mr. Twitchell has to tell us about consumer desire and meaning. But first, my personal story of seeking meaning through consumption.

I love to spend a few weeks each winter hiking and camping in the Sonoran and Mohave Deserts and a month or so in the summer doing the same in the high-mountain Colorado Rockies. I spend a lot of time dreaming about this when I am not actually doing it. I see myself as a botanizer and photographer of wildflowers and landscapes in deserts and high mountain meadows of stunning natural beauty. To do this I need equipment and I need to get there. Navigating the desert or getting up rough mountain roads to trailheads is eased with a four-wheel drive vehicle, and now that I am officially old, what could be better than a Toyota RAV4. This I came to describe as my mountain camping car, partly to assuage

---

[5]James B. Twitchell, *Lead Us into Temptation: The Triumph of the American Dream* (New York: Columbia University Press, 1999).

my guilt over owning a vehicle that gets only pretty good mileage. You might think that I bought this car to project a certain public image, but I have since determined I did it as a matter of self-definition. Driving it around any time of year made me feel like the hiker and camper I am. A piece of my self-creation is what I drive, but in my own eyes, not so much the eyes of others. I subsequently discovered that most drivers of a RAV4 use it more for going to the mall, judging from their body shapes, than driving up mountains to trailheads. Owning such a car for me symbolized my freedom to explore and have adventures, something that I doubt others perceive. There are lots of other little self-expressive things I buy that have little to do with my public image. I love the small, lightweight stuff that eases the task of backpacking like little stoves, little tents, lightweight sleeping bags, and so on. This is a REI-based (the premier outdoor store and cooperative) consumerism that helps to define who I am. I have just recently, for example, discovered moisture-wicking t-shirts that I just love. For a while, I put my consumer effort into having car camping comfort goods such as a larger tent, chairs, and a screened porch around the picnic table, all of which I have come to enjoy in my old age. I have even looked at some of the smaller travel trailers, but, like Diderot's robe, buying one would lead to still other needs, like a bigger, more powerful car.

Recently, I experienced a modest transformation in my attitude toward all this. I still absolutely love the idea of high mountain exploration even though I am slowing down in my dotage and cutting out backpacking, but I now see car ownership as a pain and driving on four wheel drive roads as creating more anxiety than pleasure. My RAV4 has been sold to my son, a big guy that has to squeeze to get into smaller vehicles and at 26 had yet to own a car (he needs it more than I), and my wife and I get along now on just one car, a gas-sipping Toyota Prius C (the baby Prius). To get deep into the mountains I will rent something or hitch a ride, and I am scaling my car camping back to mostly backpacking sized equipment that will fit on a plane and in the Prius. I have recently purchased a new camera though with a larger image sensor and a good lens for wildflower photography. There is always something more to buy. In any case, self-creation and the search for meaning is a dynamic process, and the REIs of the world do a great job selling me objects of my dreams.[6]

Academics jump on commercial consumerism as a mindless popular caving into Madison Avenue psychological manipulation motivated by a corporate conspiracy to maximize business profits. A mass production economy, capable of creating through the magic of advanced technology a cornucopia of material goods, requires for survival a mass consumption economy able to absorb all that is produced. Inadequate demand would doom such an economy to stagnation and depression. To prevent this, goods must do more than just stimulate people to consume beyond basic need. To transform the ordinary into objects of desire, the practice of marketing adds meaning to products that inherently lack it through advertising, packaging, branding, and fashion. When we buy goods, we gain not just something that is materially functional, but something that gives spark and significance to our lives. "And what could ever be wrong with that?", Twitchell rhetorically asks of us. What exactly is the problem with creating self-identity and expressing what's especially important to us through the brands of goods we voluntarily choose to possess? Isn't true democracy the right to choose whatever we want to consume absent substantial harm to others?

In order for goods to express something beyond their physical being, they must possess an identifiable brand to which a meaning can be attached. An ad at the bottom of the *New York Times* business page caught my eye a few years ago (April 13, 2011) as expressing visually and in text ideas to emotionally attract readers to a particular brand. Pictured in the ad is Breitling's Superocean watch at $3,335 along with a picture of a diver poking his shaved head in swimming goggles above water with the nearby text, "Herbert Nitsch, Airline Pilot, Deepsea Diver, Extreme Record Breaker." The diver and the watch stand out in stark contrast to a dramatic black background. The ad tells us that people who are

---

[6] Just last year our youngest son got a new job that required a car for commuting, so my wife and I sold him our Corolla. We now own a "baby" Prius C as I just explained, and have figured out how to jam into it all our camping stuff and do our mountain camping and hiking routine. Getting to trail heads is more challenging, but everything worked out in our first attempt in the summer of 2014. Our consumer self-identity is now wrapped up in getting 55 mpg in the mountains.

athletic, accomplished, powerful, heroic, affluent, and discerning in their tastes own such luxuries as Superocean underwater watches. Advertisements cannot be overly complicated or they fail in their task to attract viewers and potential customers. Very quickly we learn from the Breitling ad that someone with heroic qualities endorses the watch. If we aspire to the values and virtues the ad communicates, then we may well give serious consideration to purchasing such a watch, if we can afford it, and even if we never go diving. By acquiring the watch, we, in effect, endorse what it symbolizes in the ad, not only for our own sense of identity, but for the sake of admiring others we wish to impress who know about Breitling, which, as the ad tells us, supplies "instruments for professionals." A life of meaning for most of us amounts to choosing our heroes, and advertising endorsements facilitate this task.

As Twitchell would no doubt argue, advertising adds meaning to goods they intrinsically lack. Look at any advertisement, and I am sure you can discern the intended message conveyed about virtues of the brand and the people who consume it. Advertising and branding together take over from religion much of the means for satisfying our hopes. Prayer to gods as the path to getting what we want out of life gets displaced in the world of commerce by the magical power of goods. Nothing is more amazing to me than my iPhone that connects me to the world and allows me to socially interact with anyone I know with a touch of the screen. It also permits me to record my thoughts and ideas when I am relaxing in a Rocky Mountain meadow campsite far from civilization, and even read a book, as long as my battery lasts. It's not just advertising in a world of high technology that gives a product meaning, but the design details as well. We want an iPhone not just because of its attractive ads, but to experience all the wonderful things it can do for us. Just like prayer, commerce will get you into heaven, but it will be a heaven on earth.

One might think that a mass production economy and its capacity to produce cheaply huge numbers of identical goods would lead to us all consuming the same things and in the process creating highly similar personal identities. Through the wonders of competition in advertising, branding, product design, packaging, and fashion, diversity prevails in the consumer world. Go to any mall, or cruise the Internet, and you will discover a never-ending panoply of goods. We all have plenty to choose from in creating our own special form of life. Branding seems to refute the notion of consumer individuality since many of us select the same identical product. If enough of us didn't for a given brand, it wouldn't survive. Consuming a particular brand isn't a creative act so much as selecting a combination of brands to consume. Through choosing an ever-changing basket of brands we continuously seek identity and self-creative meaning. We brand ourselves and construct a coherent self-image by consuming a constellation of products. Life must cohere as Diderot found out in the purchase of his new robe. For those of you who don't know the story, Diderot lived a messy life including the wearing of a robe that was little more than a rag, which he decided was just too much. He thus acquired a rather plush new one that made the rest of his surroundings look even more tawdry. Soon he bought entirely new furnishings to match his new robe. In the consumer world, buying one thing inevitably leads to another. Diderot in modern terminology branded himself by creating a coherent fashion. How do we today learn about this process? Twitchell tells us it's TV that does the job, but I suspect that currently it's more than that, given the rising use of the Internet, especially by the young.

In the end, what different types of branded products do for us is what matters. Some of what products achieve is magical, yet mundanely functional. Advil gets rid of our aches and pains, Tide gets our cloths clean, Cheerios keep our heart in shape, and Coke tastes good. We feel more sensual with exotic perfume or aftershave on, and as a result we probably behave more sensually and increase our attractiveness to others. An expensive watch communicates our wealth and power in society. Fancy cars do the same while also giving us an environment of comfort and luxury and a powerful machine that can go from 0 to 60 in nothing flat. Both watches and cars rise to the status of works of art, as can a tastefully appointed living room, or a diamond bracelet. A Green Bay Packer sweatshirt in Wisconsin expresses an affiliation that connects one socially to numerous others. A Northface jacket symbolizes the outdoor activity the wearer presumably undertakes. Goods are, and always have been, signals and signs to others as well as ourselves about who we are, what we believe, and what brings meaning in our lives. Above all, goods communicate. So how does this all relate to the way we choose to arrange ourselves in space?

***

At the mid-Twentieth Century, middle-class Americans everywhere turned their backs on the old, established central cities as places to live, and they did this for good reasons. Streets were traffic-clogged, city governments were often corrupt, crime was fearsome, the quality of schools was in decline, the air was often polluted, the streets were noisy, housing was densely packed and overcrowded, and low-income immigrants of a different race were arriving daily. By contrast the suburbs looked like a dream—open green spaces, new, detached single family houses that one could own, local control of government, social and racial homogeneity, and the ability to commute to work in the privacy of one's car. What could be better?

Before World War II, cities retained the hub-and-spoke shape and relatively high density given them by the electric streetcar. People either walked to work or they rode the trolley, and many lived compactly in apartments or other kinds of multifamily housing. Outward spreading of the relatively well off to new "streetcar suburbs" for single-family housing occurred in all large cities, but population densities stayed relatively high. The economic and cultural heart and soul of the city remained at its center, but all this was about to change.[7]

Americans could have followed the prewar approach of basing the shape of urban space on public mass transit and compact housing, but they chose a distinctly different path—the creation of an urban transportation system and access to suburban housing rooted in a love affair with the automobile. A majority of urban Americans now live in suburbs instead of central cities and reside in locally governed, low-density municipalities and commute from detached single family homes to low rise business and commercial buildings surrounded by convenient parking. In the process, most Americans now avoid ever setting foot in a high-density central city. Not only did people move to the suburbs, but along with them

---

[7]Douglas E. Booth, *The Coming Good Boom: Creating Prosperity for All and Saving the Environment through Compact Living* (Charleston: Create Space, 2010).

so have businesses. The multistory central city factory located on a rail line or near a dock found itself replaced by a low-rise suburban plant with its truck bays and close access to freeways. Densely packed older department stores and high-rise offices in the central city business district have been out-competed by low-rise suburban shopping malls and office parks with their ample parking and close proximity to housing developments. Only in the suburbs could our new postwar consumer dream of possessing spacious, well appointed single-family dwellings and sleek, powerful motor vehicles be easily satisfied. Nothing is more important in symbolizing our material accomplishments than our homes and our cars. We fill our living spaces with those consumer items that define who we are, and choose motor vehicles that reflect our deepest values in life. In the U.S., what matters most is where one lives and what one drives. Governments at all levels supported and fostered this dream with home loans guaranteed against default, tax deductions for mortgage interest payments, and massive systems of freeways and highways that eased the task of moving around the suburban landscape.

For several decades following World War II, suburban expansion and the industries it fueled pumped up consumer and investment spending and assured national economic prosperity. Especially for the U.S., the passion for financial accomplishment and material goods has taken a distinctly and even radically suburban form. In our most recent economic crisis from which we are now only beginning to recover, the suburban dream faced serious challenges from an unprecedented "middle-class" experience of extraordinary housing foreclosure rates and exceptionally high unemployment levels. Our economy seriously needs a new engine of growth. The question we now want to address is whether a shift in attitudes and values is in the cards that will in itself push us toward an economy rooted in a less materialistic, more compact and environmentally friendly form of living, and whether that shift will offer us sufficient options for getting a living.

5 The Turn to Downtown Living

To set the stage for a post-material form of economic thought, let's begin with the details of an important new trend that tells us a lot about where our economic life looks to be headed: the return to compact downtown living.

***

Anyone, such as the young, 1940s-era Parisian author, playwright, and philosopher, Jean-Paul Sartre, whose passions in life require a cheap place to live, inexpensive and efficient public transit, cafes where one can linger all day for the price of a cup of coffee, personal interaction with likeminded others, access to highly specialized audiences or markets for the fruits of one's labor, or public institutions, such as museums, theaters, stadiums, gymnasiums, universities, or libraries, will be attracted to high density urban living. It is in densely packed older cities where such needs are best satisfied. Add to this a decent nightlife, good restaurants, bustling and architecturally interesting neighborhoods, and attractive parks where one can enjoy a bit of nature, and you have most of the ingredients of an "urban" as opposed to a "suburban" dream.

In my own city, two older, densely populated neighborhoods, Riverwest just to the north of downtown and Bayview just to the south, contain a mix of century-old, moderate single family houses, duplexes, and apartments, and numerous aging commercial and industrial buildings. These two neighborhoods have become havens for students, artists, activists, teachers, and a variety of others whose aspirations or incomes preclude living in the suburbs. Riverwest is the birthplace of the Lakefront Brewery, a successful producer of microbrews, and Bayview is home to innovative storefront cultural venues such as the Alchemist Theater. In both neighborhoods, one can find great new restaurants, cafes, bars, art galleries, organic food cooperatives, and funky stores. Colectivo, a rapidly growing local coffee roaster, a few years ago constructed an architecturally innovative roasting facility and cafe in Riverwest, and recently opened a huge, visually stunning new cafe in Bayview with a big bakery in view of customers who get to watch the action. Bayview is blessed with close access to a beautiful Lake Michigan shoreline park, and Riverwest borders great hiking trails along a revitalized natural Milwaukee River corridor. Riverwest is also less than a mile from the University of Wisconsin-Milwaukee (UWM) campus. Owning and using an automobile in these neighborhoods is a pain given the scarcity of parking, and one can get around easily walking or biking. Milwaukee lacks fancy light rail for public transit, but does have a fairly functional bus system. Residents of Riverwest or Bayview don't really need to bear the expense of car ownership, and they can reside in fairly decent housing more cheaply than in Milwaukee's suburbs. Crime remains a problem, but it is on the decline in both neighborhoods. If you aspire to the materialist amenities of the suburban dream, Riverwest and Bayview aren't for you. But if you are looking beyond financial accomplishment and material possessions for meaning in life, either of these neighborhoods just might be the place you would want to live.[1]

It isn't only the offbeat older neighborhoods of Milwaukee that are on the rebound, but more upscale developments in and around downtown as well, such as the city's Third Ward, an old wholesale district with architecturally unique buildings dating from the late Nineteenth Century. Here rising urban popularity has stimulated conversions of older buildings to offices and middle class dwellings, with street level retailing, alongside new condominium construction. Young, affluent professionals and suburban expats drive this trend and they seem more interested in luxury consumption than the residents of Bayview or Riverwest judging from the pricy boutiques and expensive restaurants springing up in the Third Ward and elsewhere downtown. The Third Ward hosts a public market and a performing arts complex, home to the Skylight Opera and two theater companies that specialize in modern and experimental plays. Today, the revitalized Third Ward attracts both upscale local residents and tourists to its galleries, restaurants, bars, and entertainment venues, although at the sacrifice of some of its original seedy charm.

---

[1] Tom Tolan, *Riverwest: A Community History* (Milwaukee: Past Press, 2003); Harold A. Perkins, "Green Spaces of Self-Interest Within Shared Urban Governance," *Geography Compass* 4(2010); J. Zimmerman, "From Brew Town to Cool Town: Neoliberalism and the Creative City Development Strategy in Milwaukee," *Cities* 25, no. 4 (2008).

The essential virtue of compact urban living is close spatial proximity to diverse, interesting urban neighborhoods and a variety of public and private enterprises including theaters, markets, libraries, parks, and institutions of higher learning. The fundamental advantage of expansive suburban living is the comforts of space manifested in big houses and yards, wide roads, and large, auto-accessible shopping malls. The suburbs facilitate material aspirations; diverse densely packed cities foster a broad spectrum of pursuits, some material in orientation, and some not. Great cities of the world contain their temples of consumption filled with material treasures for the wealthy, but they also contain wonderful street markets and numerous small enterprises where the desires of the palate and other simple pleasures find satisfaction at a reasonable price. One needn't be affluent to enjoy the virtues of high-density urban living and to follow a post-materialist path through life, but if you are a prosperous professional or retiree more interested in stimulating experiences than consumer acquisition, and require or desire close proximity to like-minded others, then the downtown living may well be for you.

***

Richard Florida, a regional science professor, has gained star standing among urban planners for his book, *The Rise of the Creative Class*.[2] Florida presents evidence for the emergence of an economically important group of individuals who play a driving role in a renaissance of downtown urban revitalization and have a new take on life that bears the marks of post-materialist thinking. According to Florida, this creative class is compose of professionals, such as scientists, engineers, university professors, poets, novelists, entertainers, designers, architects, and opinion-makers who conceive new intellectual or artistic forms of economic or public value. Its members are at once bohemian and conformist, like the employees at Google and Facebook we talked about earlier. They have an intense desire for personal self-expression, which includes body-piercing jewelry and tattoos, but also possess a powerful work ethic and passion for personal accomplishment, especially in the digital arena doing software

---

[2]Richard Florida, *The Rise of the Creative Class: And How It's Transforming Work, Leisure, Community and Everyday Life* (New York: Basic Books, 2002).

development or graphic arts. These are the people one increasingly sees sitting around gourmet coffee shops huddled over their computers or conversing in small groups about website design, solving a computer software problem, pulling off the conversion of an old commercial building into condominiums, or getting someone elected to political office. They don't like bureaucratic hierarchy, but believe strongly in being recognized for their work on its creative merits. They especially believe in social diversity of all kinds, and feel comfortable working with others of different races or sexual orientations. Members of the creative class both work and play hard, and express only limited interest in accumulating material possessions and are especially oriented to consuming individual and shared "experiences" such as adventure travel, road biking or rock climbing or other vigorous activities, offbeat theater performances, cutting edge studio art, or experimental musical events. While Silicon Valley is a suburban bastion for such individuals, they increasingly find urban centers such as downtown San Francisco, Seattle, or Minneapolis to be exciting places to live and work.

Youthful creative types, along with the return of aging suburban expats, fuel much of the boom in condominium construction and conversion of distinctive older commercial buildings to residences in downtowns around the country. Both groups are attracted to the excitement of urban street life in neighborhoods with concentrations of trendy restaurants, theaters, art galleries, espresso shops, brew pubs, bookstores, and entertainment venues. Retailing matters, but its orientation is to specialty foods or wines, boutiques, and outdoor stores that serve the active life of the new inner city residents.

The interest of affluent young professionals in downtown living finds confirmation in a Brookings Institution study of census data by Eugenie Birch, Professor of City and Regional Planning at the University of Pennsylvania.[3] In a sample of 44 cities, downtown population grew by ten percent in the 1990s and the number of households expanded 13 percent, a substantial recovery after years of decline. In 2000 25 to 34 year olds compose a quarter

---

[3]Eugenie L. Birch, "Who Lives Downtown?," (Washington D.C.: Brookings Institution, 2005).

of downtown populations, up from 13 percent 30 years earlier. The proportion of downtowners having a bachelor's degree rose to 44 percent by 2000, a figure that exceeds both that for cities as a whole and their suburbs. The young and the educated moving downtown are exactly those groups where post-material values predominate.

Critics of this new post-industrial urban economy argue that the return of affluent residents to the inner city has done little to alleviate the poverty that prevails in many of its neighborhoods.[4] The aggregate economy of many central cities continues to sink despite renewed economic energy in their downtowns, and little progress has been made in revitalizing central city school systems. To have a shot at entering affluent and creative occupations in the long-run, inner city residents need education, and to survive and improve their condition in the short-run, they need job training and jobs. The presence of affluent professionals and empty nesters doubtlessly stimulate service sector employment and unskilled work in building rehab and construction, but without bolstering the minimum wage[5] and improving access to decent health care, such jobs will not lead to much real economic progress among the inner city poor. In the longer haul, a strengthening of an affluent middle class who want to raise families in the inner city may create the political conditions necessary for central city educational reform to the benefit of all residents, but there is little evidence of this occurring as yet (Chicago and New York are among the many cities making an attempt at serious educational reform). A concerted public effort to reduce climatic warming by switching to a clean energy economy and compact forms of living could bring a wide range of employment opportunities to central city residents in such fields as clean energy equipment fabrication, light rail construction, and commercial and residential energy conservation, but movement in this direction has stalled for now.[6]

---

[4]Zimmerman, "From brew town to cool town: Neoliberalism and the creative city development strategy in Milwaukee."; Judith T. Kenny and Jeffrey Zimmerman, "Constructing the 'Genuine American City': Neo-traditionalism, New Urbanism and Neo-Liberalism in the Remaking of Downtown Milwaukee," *Cultural Geographies* 11(2003).
[5]Raising the minimum wage is a popular local referendum issue around the country in the 2014 election. See Barro, Josh. "Voters Will Decide Minimum Wages in Four States Tuesday." New York Times, November 3, 2014.
[6]Booth, *The Coming Good Boom: Creating Prosperity for All and Saving the*

Critics also point out that Richard Florida's use of the term "creativity" to define a social class suffers from the problem of being too nebulous to be of much practical use.[7] Given the opportunity, almost anyone can exercise creativity in their work from the espresso barista who finds a unique way to pull a better shot, to a high-tech computerized machine tool operator who develops a new procedure for improving product quality, to a roofer who figures out a better technique for installing unobtrusive venting pleasing to the eye. It's not just an elite class of youthful software code writers, web designers, and graphic artists living in affluent downtown neighborhoods who are creative. So are the custom coffee roasters, microbrewery operators, gourmet bakers, and chocolatiers springing up in Milwaukee and most other central cities who often locate in rehabbed storefronts or old factory buildings. The rebirth of this kind of manufacturing in the central city occurs in those industries where the public increasingly demands the kind of quality and uniqueness large corporations are incapable of achieving. Creativity in the world of work need not be confine to a class of youthful professionals who value freedom, diversity, and self-expression. The aspiration and potentiality to be creative in some realm of one's life is a universal one unrestricted by occupation.

***

While the critics of a rising urban post-material professional class are right about a limited public concern with the problem of central city poverty, they have missed the rise of a modest income creative class as a driving force in the central city economy. Not all the creative occupations referred to by Florida in his writings enjoy the affluence of the creative class as a whole. True creativity doesn't necessarily bring wealth as the artists of the world historically discover repeatedly. Yet it is this group that concentrates most heavily among all occupations in the central city today and serves as a driving force for neighborhood renewal.[8] The popular image of starving artists or aspiring actors living in garrets

---

Environment through Compact Living. Chapters 5-9.

[7] Ann Markusen and Greg Schrock, "The Artistic Dividend: Urban Artistic Specialisation and Economic Development Implications," *Urban Studies* 43, no. 10 (2006).

[8] Ibid.; E. Strom, "Artist Garret as Growth Machine? Local Policy and Artist Housing in U.S. Cities," *Journal of Planning Education and Research* 29, no. 3 (2010).

and waiting tables for their living stands up to academic scrutiny. Artists (defined broadly to include actors and directors, announcers, architects, drama and music teachers, authors, dancers, designers, musicians and composers, painters, sculptors, craft artists and printmakers, and photographers), in comparison to other professionals, are highly educated but poorly paid. They often hold multiple jobs in a given year, work outside their chosen occupation to make ends meet, face frequent periods of unemployment, and contend with an income distribution highly skewed towards the relatively few who experience substantial success. Financial accomplishment as an artist is a 'winner take all' gamble that very few achieve. Nonetheless, the number of artists has grown more than twice as fast as the labor force in recent decades, reflecting an expansion in public demand for the products and experiences artists have to offer as a well as a continued willingness of many artists to endure a lower income for the intrinsic rewards of creative work.[9]

Given their economic vulnerability, artists normally choose to locate in inner city neighborhoods with inexpensive rents. For those who require studios or places to rehearse, declining, seedy commercial or industrial areas often provide affordable space in which to both work and live. Artists concentrate in central cities to a greater degree than most other occupations and tend to cluster together in neighborhoods that best suit their needs for expansive but cheap workspace, artistic community connections, and access to customers. Clustering enables interactions, from which spring ideas and information on economic opportunities, and the concentration of supporting art galleries and display spaces or performance venues. Over the last forty years, Chicago's Wicker Park neighborhood has evolved into what sociologist Richard Lloyd calls a "neo-bohemia" that originated in artistic clustering.[10] The neighborhood initially offered aspiring artists and entertainers abundant older, unoccupied commercial spaces and working class bars as outlets for performers as well as watering holes for the

---

[9]Neil O. Alper and Gregory H. Wassall, "Artists' Careers and their Labor Markets," in *Handbook of the Economics of Art and Culture*, ed. Victor A. Ginsburgh and David Throsby (Amsterdam: North-Holland, 2006).
[10]Richard Lloyd, *Neo-Bohemia: Art and Commerce in the Postindustrial City* (New York: Routledge, 2006).

invading "bohemians." By the late 1990s in Wicker Park, numerous trendy restaurants, bars, entertainment venues, coffee shops, and art galleries emerged to serve Chicago's growing class of affluent young professionals. Along with this came a flood of building rehabs and condo construction that pushed property values dramatically upward, driving many of the artists that set off the whole process in the first place to cheaper rents on the neighborhood's periphery.

For Wicker Park, artistic vitality turned out to be self-destructive as it has for other so called bohemian communities such as Paris' Montmartre or Left Bank or San Francisco's North Beach. Post-materialist young professionals attracted to downtown living retain some of the consumerist tendencies of their affluent parents, but turn more to spending their dollars on shared experiences as opposed to the accumulation of material possessions, and they love doing so in a neo-bohemian bastion of creativity. They choose to live at high densities in condos and apartments for the privilege of participating in the varieties of human experience that requires proximity—music and entertainment, art galleries and public art, museums and the performance arts, and a lusty bar scene. Life on the streets and in the parks of a big city in itself constitutes a human drama that the suburbs are challenged to match. Part of the charm of neighborhoods like Wicker Park is their marginality and the oddballs and characters they attract. Suburbs are safe and convenient while the central city is dangerous but exciting and stimulating. The problem with the invasion of affluence into neighborhoods like Wicker Park is the pushing out of those people who create the bohemian ambience in the first place.[11]

While a local neighborhood arts scene may be attractive to affluent consumers, gentrification need not be the inevitable result. Milwaukee's Riverwest, with 11,500 residents just to the north of downtown, has evolved recently into a local arts and entertainment center with a growing collection of interesting bars and restaurants. Settled more than a century ago, working class immigrant Polish families originally built modest duplexes and small simple frame

---

[11]Ibid.; Richard Lloyd, "Neo-Bohemia: Art and Neighborhood Redevelopment in Chicago," *Journal of Urban Affairs* 24(2002).

houses in Riverwest that continue to exist to this very day. The neighborhood also contains a variety of old storefronts and a number of aging factory buildings. Artists usually rent their dwellings, but one of the big attractions of Riverwest is the feasibility of purchasing a modest house or storefront that can serve as both a studio and a place to live. The humble character of the housing stock gives it an immunity from gentrification and keeps the neighborhood affordable and attractive not just to artists, but to a racially and ethically diverse collection of residents as well as students from nearby UWM. For the past twenty-seven years, the Riverwest Artists Association has sponsored ArtWalk, a walking tour displaying the creations of a hundred plus local artists at studios, galleries, and homes throughout the neighborhood, demonstrating the scale and endurance of the local arts community. If anyone expresses post-materialist values, it is artists, and alongside the arts community in Riverwest exist a number of activists groups with goals beyond material accomplishment, including the Riverwest Neighborhood Association, Peace Action Center, Riverwest Rainbow Alliance (an organization of gay, lesbian, bisexual, and transgender residents), and Children's Outing Association. While the occupants of expensive condos along the Milwaukee River on the southern edge of Riverwest may well be seeking post-materialist consumer experiences in the central city, Riverwest residents hue to a more fully fledged post-materialist philosophy in their economic sacrifices for the sake of creative expression. Nonetheless, there is a certain economic symmetry in Riverwest's durability as an arts community and the springing up of affluent condo development nearby. Riverwest has artistic experiences and objects to sell, and the young professionals and suburban expats moving into nearby condos have the money to buy.[12]

***

The return of an affluent middle class to the central city in places like Chicago's Wicker Park and Milwaukee's Third Ward reflects a growing post-materialist interest in experiences that require "shared consumption." When we share we get pulled outside of self-concern. This is especially the case with such events

---

[12]Tolan, *Riverwest: A Community History*.

as musical performances, theatrical presentations, visual art displays, sporting events, and political pep rallies. In such instances, being a part of an audience or participatory group is an integral part of the experience. The same is true more casually in the enjoyment of a neighborhood's street or cafe life, or on a Sunday stroll through a park or along an urban lakeshore. In all such instances the private possession of goods by the consumer is immaterial to the experience. Artists in central cities, who are themselves paragons of post-materialist self-creation, acquire an economic niche by virtue of their ability to serve a post-materialist shift in the nature of middle class consumption. Artists survive by producing opportunities for experience. Post-materialist experience requires proximity, and compact living greases the skids of spatial proximity and promotes the sharing of experiences in both public and private spaces. It is in urban spaces where we get our fullest exposure to the diversity of the human experience, and where we have the greatest opportunity to submerge our personal egos in the content and flow of this larger reality. This is not to say that post-materialism lacks its dangers. The urban entertainment industry is driven partly by a dark Dionysian alcohol and drug fueled desire for ecstatic group experiences and sexual unions that can have exploitative and addictive outcomes, especially for those doing the work of serving (see the next chapter for more on this problem). Aspiring artists pushed into part-time service work out of economic necessity often have to put up with obnoxious and even violent behavior for the sake of getting tips, and can get stuck doing work for much of their lives they didn't plan on. The post-materialist values of the young urban professional remain a mixture of hedonistic desire for urban entertainment and a self-transcendent interest in creativity and human diversity. Underlying this, nonetheless, lays a real passion for the products of human creativity. A bohemia without creativity along with its lusty and tragic qualities wouldn't be much of a bohemia. Artistic creativity ultimately produces objects and experiences that give insight into existential meaning. The post-materialism of young professionals may lack seriousness and for many may only be vicarious, but it does nonetheless support living more compactly in the service of human creativity.

Philosophy matters. For nearly a century now our human spatial dream has been materialist, spatially expansive, and suburban, but the winds of our dreams may now be subtly shifting toward a post-materialist philosophy and high density urban compactness that better serves post-material needs. We normally think of philosophy as something for academics to argue about, but it is more important than that. Our philosophical outlook lies behind how we live in the world, and a shift in the values by which we live can change the way we live.

A modest trend towards city living may not seem like much, but if it continues it will be a big deal. A shift to living at higher densities may well come in the nick of time to help reverse our ominous march to climatic warming. If you live in a densely packed central city instead of a spatially expansive suburb, you move around much less to get to work, for shopping, and doing all the other things you love to do. When you do move around in the city, chances are greater that you will walk, bike, or take public transit than if you lived instead in low density suburbs where odds are that you would drive everywhere because everything is so far apart. In short, if you move from suburb to city, you will cut back on your driving and the volume of auto-related greenhouse gas emissions you cause. Also in the city, chances are you will live in a smaller dwelling that requires much less greenhouse gas-emitting energy for heat and light, and if you live in a multi-family unit and share heat-emitting exterior walls and roof areas with others, your dwelling will be much more energy efficient than a single family, low rise house in the suburbs. By deciding to live in the city, you will do the environment a big favor whether you think much about it or not. If you are a post-material environmentalist, you might even decide to live in the city to live out your own philosophical values apart from realizing the benefits of city living. Again, philosophy is not just for the ivory tower but really matters in everyday life. A post-material future will differ from the materialist past.

6 Starving Artists and Their Existential Problem

Invariably, every new social phenomenon has its "dark side," and this is no less the case with the turn to downtown living. We already described in the last chapter how not all the talented drivers of urban expansion Richard Florida talks about in his book, *The Rise of the Creative Class*,[1] are as lucky economically as he infers, and this leaves in its path serious social problems as we will now see. The creative talents of the Chicago arts district, Wicker Park, described by Richard Lloyd in his book *Neo-Bohemia*, struggle to make a living unlike their affluent young customers who haunt the neighborhood's galleries, espresso shops, and nightspots.[2] It is in the Wicker Park bars and music venues that actual and aspiring artists and musicians work to make ends meet. In this hip, bohemian setting, servers, who treat their physical selves as their own vehicle for artistic expression, face special challenges daily. To gain and then retain their employment, servers must project a unique persona attractive to their experience-seeking clientele. Bar and restaurant owners compete for customers through the edgy image their establishments present. As Lloyd notes, servers have to strike a balance in the hustle for tips between pleasing their customers and fending off unwanted sexual advances. Servers also face the danger of getting caught up in the nightlife culture and neglecting their larger artistic goals, going out for free drinks on their nights off supplied by counterparts in other bars instead of doing creative work. Because these less fortunate members of the creative class face the kinds of dilemmas described by Jean-Paul Sartre's existentialist philosophy, spending a little time with his ideas should help us sharpen our thinking about the realities of a newly emergent "creative class" so important to the return to compact urban living.

---

[1]Richard Florida, *The Rise of the Creative Class: And How It's Transforming Work, Leisure, Community and Everyday Life* (New York: Basic Books, 2002).
[2]Richard Lloyd, *Neo-Bohemia: Art and Commerce in the Postindustrial City* (New York: Routledge, 2006). See the discussion of Wicker Park in Chapter 5.

In *Being and Nothingness,* Sartre describes abstractly what it means to exist in the world. At a given moment we are an "in-itself," a simple object in the world like any other. As an in-itself we are no different than rocks, avocados, or snakes, or any other existent thing. But unlike non-human objects, we humans amazingly possess a consciousness with a capacity for self-recognition and reflection. Self-reflection brings forth a "for-itself" which constantly jumps ahead of what we are at any given moment (our in-itself) to think about our next move, our future actions. A constant restlessness puts us perpetually at the ready to move forward, to shift into a new and novel state of being. Here arise Sartre's notions of "not-being," negation, and nothingness. Never happy with our current condition, we keep pushing toward a desired future state. We don't have the house we want, haven't yet traveled to Australia or found the love of our life, and don't fully understand Martin Heidegger's philosophy much less Jean-Paul Sartre's. In short, we are never happy with what we are and press for something different. Our physical and mental in-itself is never up to our consciously wanted self-image. The in-itself is a thing in a certain physical state; consciousness is self-aware thought; and never the two shall meet. We live on a moving treadmill of not-yet-realized expectations from which we can never exit. We are not what we truly desire and are stuck in a special kind of nothingness—not-being what we should.[3]

Sartre's basic premise is that existence lacks intrinsic meaning, and we are here in the world for no obvious reason. This fact gives us great freedom, intense anguish, and a huge responsibility. We have no alternative but to choose a path through life—we are "condemned to be free" as Sartre puts it. The life we choose is up to us and we bear the responsibility for how it turns out. Our fear that we will lack the courage to exercise our choice responsibly and authentically creates in us a deep anguish. Many of us try to avoid this by adopting roles and meanings in life that society coughs up for us—the tried and the true, the socially acceptable. Even then, subconscious doubt about what we should do and be will remain, causing us to continue in a vague and undefined state

---

[3]Jean-Paul Sartre, *Being and Nothingness* (New York: Washington Square Press, 1992).

of anguish. If we go with the popular flow, we fall into a life of self-delusion and bad faith about who we are and really want to be.

Sartre has little use for bourgeois conformity and oppressive conventions, a view he expresses through the principle character, Rouquentin, in his best-selling first novel, *Nausea,* set in Bouville, a fictional commercial seaport on the French coast. While looking enviously on the fact that members of the Bouville middle class possess well defined life projects that supply them with a self-identity and meaning in the form of family, home, and profession, Rouquentin finds the repeated routines he observes in the life of the town as tedious and boring, even repellent. The presence of those nauseating others he observes around him with their socially determined projects forces Rouquentin to look honestly at his own life. He finds the historical research that he works on daily in the local library to be useless and comes to see the world around him as absurd and alienating and his own life to be an empty failure. The problem for him is an absence of meaning in his work, relationships with others, and the environment around him. Until the very end of the book, he can't see his way out. His conscious self doesn't know how to direct his being to a meaningful existence. Only in the final pages is there a glimmer of hope in his decision to move to Paris and write a novel (kind of like Sartre).[4]

The biggest pitfall we face in the quest for a life of meaning, Sartre tells us, is the danger of caving into society's demands for conformity and submission to social judgment. A lack of self-confidence in our own ability to choose a life-path causes us to look to our fellow human beings for acknowledgement, but we should do so with trepidation. Normal human affection—a relaxed and unthreatening felt connection to someone else—gets suppressed by the judgmental "look of the other," that "evil eye" projected on those who do wrong, calling for them to shrink in shame. The fear of social judgment holds out the danger of failing to be who we authentically want to be.

Consider the actions of a typical Parisian waiter as describe by Sartre in *Being and Nothingness*: "His movement is quick and forward, a little too precise, a little too rapid. He comes toward the patron with a step a little too quick. He bends forward a little too

---

[4] Jean-Paul Sartre, *Nausea* (New York: New Directions, 2007).

eagerly; his voice, his eyes express an interest a little too solicitous for the order of the customer...All his behavior seems to us a game."[5]

Sartre wrote this to illustrate the notion of "bad faith," the idea that we play at our role and do so to conform to practices demanded by the public. We get diverted by social requirements into adopting a pattern of life rather than creating one that is uniquely our own. We delude ourselves into thinking we act freely when in reality we succumb to the perceived judgment of others. In Sartre's eyes, social life boils down to an exploitive dance in which we fruitlessly try to control each other's perceptions. In the end, failure dooms us in such attempts. We can never really know our real influence on the true feelings of others. Rather than getting on with our own self-chosen authentic projects, in Sartre's view we waste our energies in the mutual pursuit of strategic and conflicting ends in our personal relationships. Whether he is right, I leave for you to judge. I can imagine other possibilities, such as something like the following.

Return for a moment to a Parisian cafe. Waiters follow traditional patterns in their work that comply with public expectations, but this does not rule out creative and unique interpretations of what it is to be a waiter. One can imagine a waiter doing his work in a way that authentically expresses his own idiosyncratic personality. A tall, handsome waiter of Haitian extraction glides to my table, inquires as to my well being, takes my order and magically appears moments later with my double espresso and croissant, placing them precisely and gently on the table while commenting on the beauty of the day. The man behaves with pride in his profession, something I can appreciate and enjoy. He spends time with each customer, some whom seem to be friends from the neighborhood who interact with him on a basis of equality and mutual respect. He later returns to collect my money, making change with dignity and efficiency. The next day I return for a repeat performance. This time a customer, who is elegantly dressed, looks wealthy, and probably comes regularly, sits down in the cafe several minutes after me. The waiter, aware of the circumstances, serves me first despite the obvious

---

[5] Sartre, *Being and Nothingness*. Page 101.

impatience of the snooty regular. This is what a good waiter does as a matter of practice, refraining from any strategic judgment about ultimate rewards in deciding whom to serve first. We don't see the whole of our Haitian waiter in our brief interactions, but we do see at least part of his life that seems to honestly express who he is.

One could take this alternative interpretation of a waiter's life too far. No occupation is an entirely a thorn-free bed of roses. Customers can be difficult, muscles will ache after a long day, and repetitious tasks can be tedious. Still, one sees pride in the affectations of at least some waiters who indeed perform for us, but who do so with authenticity and real concern. Participating creatively in the tradition of a Parisian waiter could be a consciously and freely chosen activity, much like writing *Being and Nothingness*. The question for us here is whether the freedoms in behavior enjoyed by our Haitian waiter, or for that matter of a book-writing Jean-Paul Sartre, extends to the artists and servers of Wicker Park.

The heyday of arts community predominance in Wicker Park occurred in the 1990s prior to an influx of young, affluent professionals into the area. A few of the bars were already emerging as entertainment venues for rock bands who attracted outsiders into the neighborhood, but most of the cafes and watering holes were oriented to a local clientele. By 2000, the neighborhood had become a cultural and entertainment destination with and expanding array of restaurants, bars, galleries, antique stores, and boutiques depending largely on a youngish, affluent clientele. At this point developers became active in the area constructing new housing for upper income customers. While rising rents pushed some artists to the neighborhood's periphery, the area retains its bohemian and hip flavor even though the local population mix has shifted decidedly in favor of those who work in Chicago's downtown business establishment. Digitally tuned-in local artistic talents has attracted a number of web design firms who require not only computer literacy but an aesthetic sensibility in their employees as well.[6]

---

[6] Lloyd, *Neo-Bohemia: Art and Commerce in the Postindustrial City*.

Wicker Park retains a class divide between young professionals and artists that finds its clearest expression in the neighborhood's bars that rely heavily on an influx of affluent youths seeking a Bacchanalian ecstatic experienced fueled by music, drink, drugs, and a potential for sexual liaison. The primary source of labor for local bars and restaurants is the nearby arts community whose members depend on such work for a living while pursuing entry into their chosen careers. Youth, looks, and a unique but hip fashion sense help immeasurably in getting hired as a server or bar tender in Wicker Park. Unlike the conformity to tradition of Sartre's Parisian waiter, Wicker Park servers are rewarded for an offbeat and unique style in their appearance that becomes a design element for bars and nightclubs in their competitive efforts to attract customers. Servers in this environment enjoy the opportunity of expressing their own artistic skill by creating themselves as a work of art. The downside in this form of expression is the role it plays in competition for both employment and tips. Female servers must balance success as a server and the extra tips that can come with a sexually provocative look against the problem of unwanted sexual advances from male customers as described in the previous chapter. In short, the capacity for creating a unique style is limited by the expectations of not only bar owners but tip-supplying customers as well. Just as is the case for a Parisian waiter, the work of being a Wicker Park server can be strenuous, repetitive, and at times boring. Servers, to repeat, also have to deal with social pressures from their colleagues to go out drinking in their off hours, taking away time from their artistic pursuits and downtime from the physical and mental stresses of the job. Alcohol addiction and a failure to pursue professional goals can be the end result. As one server expresses it, "If I'm still here in a year, kill me."[7]

The artistic quest can be an authentic and laudable pursuit of expressions of meaning that help to "spiritualize" the Dionysian love of life talked about by Friedrich Nietzsche in *The Birth of Tragedy*. The visual and performance arts possess the capacity to help us both celebrate and sublimate life's powerful sensual urges that can easily get out of control. Artists serve us in their work by

---

[7] Ibid.

finding, depicting, and sacralizing meaning in the experience of life, rather than in the heavens beyond. If anyone can overcome the dangers of Sartre's bad faith and anguish in choosing a path through life, artists have a good chance at it. As we see for Wicker Park servers, circumstances can nonetheless conspire against them in obtaining their hearts' desires. While they may see themselves as uniquely creative individuals, the conditions servers face can work against them in truly attaining their artistic purposes. They face a special danger of exercising a self-delusive "bad faith" by ignoring their true condition.

Whether or not the Wicker Park case constitutes a widespread phenomenon matters. If artists create urban communities that ultimately get destroyed in a gentrification process driven by an influx of post-materialist young professionals, then this new form of compact living will possess a dark and undesirable quality. While many well known urban bohemian districts have succumbed to affluence, all arts-based neighborhoods needn't suffer the same fate. Milwaukee, a seemingly ordinary older industrial city, surprisingly contains a substantial population of artists, many of whom have taken up residence in inner city neighborhoods such as Riverwest and Bayview. As already described, Riverwest houses numerous artists, art studios, interesting restaurants and bars, and a variety of entertainment venues, including the Jazz Gallery run by the Riverwest Artists Association. Riverwest serves as a local bastion of activist, left-leaning politics that attracts substantial involvement by local artists and adds a stabilizing element to the neighborhood. Despite a solid core of artists living and working in the neighborhood and earning extra income in an expanding nightlife, unlike Wicker Park, Riverwest has avoided an influx of affluent young professionals into the neighborhood and a surge in property values. Artists have been able to solidify their presence by taking up ownership of aging, affordable Polish flats, duplexes, and storefronts that have little middle class appeal but can be rendered into comfortable and pleasing spaces in which to live and work. The local nightlife lacks the supercharged energy of Wicker Park, but provides a more community oriented and less exploitive

---

[8] Tolan, *Riverwest: A Community History*.

working environment for servers and bartenders, most of whom live in the local neighborhood just like many of their customers.[8]

The experience of other cities confirms the reality of two divergent paths for the impact of the arts on urban neighborhoods. In those first tier artistic centers such as New York and San Francisco, concentrations of artists in neighborhoods often become attractors for development of the type experienced in Chicago's Wicker Park. In cities where housing pressures are less substantial such as Philadelphia or Minneapolis-St. Paul, researchers find that artists often bring neighborhood revitalization of the kind we see in Milwaukee's Riverwest without much displacement of ethnic or racial minorities.[9] Artists in these cities find urban havens in which to live and work that possess an intrinsic immunity to high-pressure gentrification and can be stabilized with the help of a little political activism. In sum, the growth of the arts profession nationally has led to local creations of moderate income but stable compact urban communities. It's not just the return to the central city of affluent professionals that drives an urban renaissance. The social and economic dynamic of a Riverwest appears to offer more opportunity than a Wicker Park for overcoming the anguish and tendency to bad faith we all face in making something of our lives. The kind of post-materialism we see taking shape in the Riverwests of the urban world as opposed to the Wicker Parks may well help us surmount the barriers to an authentic human existence raised in the philosophy of Jean-Paul Sartre and instead celebrate the wonders of our existential being.

---

[9]A. Markusen and A. Gadwa, "Arts and Culture in Urban or Regional Planning: A Review and Research Agenda," *Journal of Planning Education and Research* 29, no. 3 (2010); Ann Markusen and Greg Schrock, "The artistic dividend: Urban artistic specialisation and economic development implications," *Urban Studies* 43, no. 10 (2006).

7 Working Hours and the Creative Impulse

If the "creative impulse" is to be fully realized, it must somehow be reconciled with the world of paid work, as we see from the Wicker Park experience. To repeat one more time, meaning in life comes from adopting and pursuing purposes about which we care passionately. For most of us a substantial portion of our waking being is taken up with paid work, something we must do in order to earn an income to supply the material instruments of life. If meaning comes from materialist ends, then the purpose of work would be to make money and all else wouldn't matter. While earning an income is the predominant motive for working, the activity of work serves more functions than just merely a means to material existence.

For many of us, work is the social center of our lives. One of the most robust findings of happiness research is the importance of friendships for life satisfaction, and it's at work where we develop many of our enduring friendships that spill over into our life as a whole. Work can provide more than just money and friends if we are lucky. Truly interesting work challenges our intellectual and physical abilities and causes us to enter into a state of active engagement—what psychologists call flow—where immediate feeling-state worries evaporate. During the activity of such work, consciousness of pleasure or pain disappears, and it is only after the fact that a warm glow of satisfaction and accomplishment emerges. To top it off, work holds out the possibility of achieving those creative purposes that bring meaning to our life. It is not just the activity of work that matters to us, but the final purpose it serves as well. Of course not all work provides a full range of such benefits. Much work is tedious and boring, offers only limited opportunities for social interactions, and lacks a valued purpose. In such instances, work is undertaken for narrower ends. One could imagine a highly skilled hedge fund manager who makes millions of dollars but secretly believes the purpose of his work to be trivial or even socially destructive, or a poorly paid nursing home aide who finds the work itself to be tedious and stressful but believes it to be of high social importance.[1]

The non-economic dimensions of work take on a special importance for post-materialist young professionals. They desire work that allows them to creatively apply their talents and skills to socially valuable undertakings and they want to do this in a socially interesting environment. The recently established General Assembly, a Manhattan incubator for web application and service businesses, fills the post-materialist bill for code-writing entrepreneurs who rent glassed-off office space abutting a common room where tenants can enjoy a cup of gourmet coffee while chatting with their fellow digital pioneers about their latest web successes and failures. A startup, Yipit, an aggregator and analyzer of daily internet commerce deals, began by renting space in the General Assembly, but after successfully generating revenue flows for its services, moved to its own home in nearby office space, Ping-Pong table included.[2] We don't normally think of New York City as a high technology paradise, but it now trails only San Francisco as a haven for digital startup capital. The blending of work and leisure in New York's high tech culture is evident in the new "techie fashion shows, techie reality TV shows, techie entrepreneurs on the Council of Foreign Relations, and techie scalpers hawking tickets outside the New York Tech Meetup, the industry's premier (and perennially sold-out) monthly event." New York's "Silicon Alley" flourishes in part because of the decline of Wall Street as an attractive career path and desires by new workforce entrants to avoid being a cog in a bureaucratic wheel and to return to the tradition of "craft work" where the final product of one's efforts can be directly observed.

Such a vision of work in the new technology world may not apply universally. Zynga, a highly successful Internet gaming startup, warranted a *New York Times* article with the title, "Zynga's Tough Culture Risks a Talent Drain."[3] Frustrated workers

---

[1] Ed Diener and Martin Seligman, "Beyond Money: Toward an Economy of Well-Being," *Social Indicators Research Series* 37(2009); Alfonso Sousa-Poza and Adres A. Sousa-Poza, "Well-Being at Work: A Cross-national Analysis of the Level and Determinants of Job Satisfaction," *Journal of Socio-Economics* 29(2000).
[2] Alan Feuer, "On the Move, in a Thriving Tech Sector," *New York Times* November 19, 2011.

complain about long hours, stressful deadlines, and a relentless tracking of progress and performance. Those who don't measure up are quickly shown the door. The esprit de corp common to many Internet companies has been replaced at Zygna with an intense individualistic meritocracy, but without a serious dent in the company's economic success. While Zynga may be an outlier in its extreme methods of work organization, intense internal competition amongst employees tends to prevail in the gaming industry. Apparently there is more than one way to skin the high technology organization cat. Not all startups fulfill post-materialist workplace desires.

Research for industrialized countries on how people feel about their working life finds that most are satisfied with their jobs, but that satisfaction is higher where the work is interesting and good relations with management prevail. Opportunities for working independently and good pay also play a role in job satisfaction but fall below intrinsic work interest and good relations with the boss in importance.[4] These research findings provide backup for what Richard Florida (*The Rise of the Creative Class*) finds anecdotally in focus group conversations with "creative class" post-materialist young professionals. Post-materialists want in their work what most of us want—a degree of control, social connection, engaging activity, a sense of accomplishment, and a worthy purpose.[5]

Despite feeling satisfied with their work, some Americans are unhappy about the amount of hours in a year they actually spend on the job. About 37 percent want to work fewer hours, around 22 percent want to work more, and the rest are content with their time on the job. High incomes and a college education results in a preference for reduced working hours, contrary to anecdotal reports of creative class satisfaction with long hours.[6] Young people at Google and places like it may be happy with periods of long work hours in a fun work environment, but they are unlikely

---

[3]Evelyn M. Rusli, "Zynga's Tough Culture Risks a Talent Drain," *New York Times*, November 11, 2011.
[4]Sousa-Poza and Sousa-Poza, "Well-Being at Work: A Cross-national Analysis of the Level and Determinants of Job Satisfaction."
[5]Florida, *The Rise of the Creative Class: And How It's Transforming Work, Leisure, Community and Everyday Life*.
[6]Jeremy Reynolds, "You Can't Always Get the Hours You Want: Mismatches between Actual and Preferred Work Hours in the U.S," *Social Forces* 81, no. 4 (2003).

to want this for the whole of their working lives. The statistical reality is that a post-materialist attachment to the quality of work itself leads to a desire for fewer hours, while, unsurprisingly, a belief in the importance of earning a substantial salary results in a desire to work more hours. Materialists want more hours, post-materialist want fewer. Liking work doesn't necessarily mean you want long days on the job.

The one odd quirk in American work time preference studies occurs for working families. Working parents, who more than others face a time-bind in their daily lives due to family responsibilities, ironically desire more hours on the job. One explanation is simple and compelling—a need for higher income to meet the costs of raising a family. Another explanation is a little unexpected—a desire to escape the impositions of family existence. Despite our love for children, parental life satisfaction declines during the child rearing years according to happiness researchers.[7] While we love our children, work at times can be a respite from the challenges of parenting.

A comparison of the U.S. and European experience with work offers up a more deeply puzzling result about American work time desires. Europeans and Americans worked about the same number of hours a week per working-aged adult back in the 1970s, but since then the weekly average hours worked have declined dramatically in Europe but not in the U.S. Today the French and Germans work about three-fourths of the average weekly hours of Americans. Around a fourth of these lower European hours derive from a shorter normal workweek and the rest from a combination of more holiday and vacation days and lower workforce participation. While real income growth per hour worked follows a comparable path in the U.S. and Europe, Europeans have chosen to take economic gains in the form of fewer working hours and more leisure while Americans have not.[8]

Surveys find that Europeans experience an increase in life satisfaction as their hours of work decline. By contrast the more

---

[7] Daniel Gilbert, *Stumbling on Happiness* (New York: Knopf, 2006). Page 221.
[8] Alberto Alesina, Edward Glaeser, and Bruce Sacerdote, "Work and Leisure in the United States and Europe: Why So Different?," in *NBER Macroeconomics Annual 2005*, ed. Mark Gertler and Kenneth Rogoff (Cambridge: MIT Press, 2005).

Americans work, the proportion reporting that they are "very happy" rises slightly, while the more Europeans work, such a report declines markedly. Europeans clearly prefer to work fewer hours and spend more time seeking their satisfactions elsewhere. Americans by contrast find happiness in working more hours rather than fewer. Europeans place more value on the quality of work than Americans, while Americans value the economic results of work more than Europeans. Europeans apparently trade off the satisfactions of work against those of leisure while Americans balance the virtues of leisure against earned income. Income wins out for Americans and leisure for Europeans. As one researcher puts it, "Americans live to work while Europeans work to live."[9]

In looking at the data on post-materialist values, one would think Americans would be just like Europeans in their working-time desires. The proportion of Americans holding post-materialist values sits in the same ballpark as Europeans. Why don't Americans express their post-materialism in a preference for fewer working hours just like Europeans? While some Americans want to work less, the majority is either content with their working hours or want to work more. This is a puzzle precisely because of a comparable prevalence of post-materialist values in both the U.S. and Europe. The answer to this puzzle may well lie in a historically ironclad connection between employment and access to health insurance in the U.S.

***

A key barrier to shorter hours in the U.S. economy not found in Europe has been the way in which health insurance is delivered. In most European countries health insurance coverage is universal and funded largely through government. In the U.S. health insurance for most is tied to full-time employment and the cost is partially funded by employers as a benefit. The very poor receive health insurance from the government through Medicaid and the elderly from Medicare. Because American employers provide very limited health insurance benefits to part-time workers, many would prefer to have full-time work simply to obtain health insurance at a

---

[9]Adam Okulicz-Kozaryn, "Europeans Work to Live and Americans Live to Work (Who is Happy to Work More: Americans or Europeans)," *Journal of Happiness Studies* 12(2011).

reasonable cost. Buying health insurance in the U.S. on one's own, until the recent passage of the Affordable Health Care Act (Obamacare), has been a costly proposition. Given that health insurance benefit costs vary with the number of workers and not average hours worked, employers can often save money by hiring fewer workers at longer weekly hours to meet a given product demand. In short, the U.S. health insurance system creates a bias towards a longer average workweek and against part-time jobs with health insurance benefits. In Europe, part-time work can be chosen without sacrificing access to health insurance because of its assured availability by government, but in the U.S. few part-time jobs offer affordable health insurance.[10]

The health insurance issue takes on special importance for a key subgroup of the creative class, the starving artists. Many artists are self-employed in the U.S. and lack access to affordable health insurance. Many also supplement their income from part-time work that lacks health insurance benefits. The health insurance problem forces many American would-be artists to seek full-time work in other fields. Because European artists don't need to worry about health insurance costs, they experience greater flexibility than Americans in combining their artistic efforts with other kinds of work to supplement their incomes.[11] Until Obamacare, anyone who truly wanted to work part time in the U.S. had to contend with a lack of health insurance on top of low pay.

As the Dutch have demonstrated over the past 30 years, part-time work needn't be marginalized and relegated to a lower economic status than full-time work. The Dutch have adopted government policies that require equalized hourly pay and access to benefits for equivalent part-time and full-time work. Dutch workers also have a right to request reductions in their individual working hours with proportionate reductions in pay. Since the introduction of these reforms, the share of part-time work in the Dutch economy has increase dramatically and the hours worked per capita has decline significantly as well. The share of part-time

---

[10]Jonathan Gruber and Brigitte C. Madrian, "Health Insurance, Labor Supply, and Job Mobility: A Critical Review of the Literature," in *Working Paper 8817* (Cambridge: National Bureau of Economic Research, 2002).
[11]Alper and Wassall, "Artists' Careers and their Labor Markets."

employment in the Netherlands exceeds that for all other European countries, and the Dutch seem to be perfectly happy working less than others. Unlike American part-time workers, very few Dutch desire a shift to full-time employment. All this has been accomplished alongside economic growth and declines in unemployment.[12]

The U.S. has considerable distance to go before equalizing the status of full- and part-time work, but, with passage of the Affordable Health Care Act, part-time work in the future will look more attractive to Americans.[13] Under the Act, anyone is able to acquire health insurance policies on government-run exchanges without having to worry about denial for pre-existing medical conditions. Because the cost of such policies are to be subsidized for those with limited incomes, obtaining affordable health insurance coverage as a part-time worker is now much easier. The new health insurance reforms will benefit artists and others who seek satisfaction of their creative impulses outside of conventional full-time work and desire part-time employment to help satisfy their material needs.

Affordable health insurance will increase the appeal of lower paid but more creative work,[14] and this will in turn increase the attractiveness of compact urban neighborhoods for those who choose to pursue a post-materialist path to meaning. If full-time work were necessary for health insurance, the higher income that comes with it will make a spatially expansive, consumption-oriented life in the suburbs feasible. If you make a lot of money in less than fully satisfying full-time employment required for health insurance, then you might as well spend it on the pleasures of a comfortable house in the suburbs and the convenience of a luxury motor vehicle. But if conventional full-time work is no longer needed for health insurance, and the pursuit of one's true passion becomes possible through less remunerative activities, then the

---

[12] A. Hayden, "Work-time Reduction and the Dutch Economic Miracle," (Toronto: 32 Hours: Action for Full Employment, 1999); Jelle Visser, "The first part-time economy in the world: a model to be followed?," *Journal of European Social Policy* 12, no. 1 (2002).
[13] Annie Lowrey and Jonathan Weisman, "Health Care Law Projected to Cut the Labor Force," *New York Times*, February 4, 2014.
[14] Shaila Dewan, "How Obamacare Could Unlock Job Opportunities," *New York Times*, February 14, 2014.

likelihood of a turn to a more affordable way of life in a spatially compact setting will increase. We have already laid out key post-materialist attractions of high density urban living, such as access to lively neighborhoods, entertainment and the arts, good cuisine, and interesting architecture, but for those on a limited budget other features matter as well such as the ability to find affordable housing, use public instead of private transportation, and substitute public for private space. Life in compact cities is lived more in public arenas, such as parks, squares, libraries, and coffee houses, instead of in spacious suburban houses and big backyards. Entry to public spaces normally costs little while the ownership of private space can be expensive. Getting around densely packed cities by mass transit, on foot, or by bike is often more convenient and certainly less expensive than by motor vehicle. Post-materialism as a way of life is available not just to affluent young professionals in urban centers, but, as artists have demonstrated, for those willing to give up income in order to satisfy deeply held creative urges and values. Artists and others who seek a less materially oriented way of living have been at the forefront of carving out an affordable urban niche by revitalizing deteriorated, older central city neighborhoods. If one doesn't have to face excessive costs for access to health care, then the adoption of a truly post-materialist form of life will be significantly eased and compact living will be given a boost.

8 Philosophy Matters for Climate Change

Philosophical outlooks held by actual people, not just intellectuals, make a difference in their daily economic lives. As we have seen here, the shape of our global future is moving steadily into the hands of post-materialists who downplay narrowly economic goals in favor of self-expression, personal autonomy, and a universalist concern for the well being of both humanity and nature. Will attitudes post-materialists express towards the problem of climate change truly matter for the future? Can the clout of a politically powerful, entrenched minority of climate change deniers be overcome by a growing popular majority deeply worried about the consequences of global warming for the earth's environment? Taking a careful look at what we know about actual human attitudes on global warming should help us all form a better judgment about where our climate future is headed.

Post-materialists support for environmental improvement manifests itself both directly and inadvertently. Direct support includes choosing to live in an energy efficient dwelling for the conscious purpose of reducing carbon emissions, or voting for a senate candidate who promises to work for legislation that will limit climate change. Inadvertent support results from choices undertaken by post-materialists for purposes other than environmental improvement. A software engineer, who sells her 5,000 square foot house in Silicon Valley and gives up her job at Google in favor of a 1,000 square foot apartment in San Francisco in walking distance of her new job at a startup working on educational software for inner city students, unintentionally reduces her carbon emissions footprint by living more compactly. We already know that post-materialists lead an economic resurgence occurring in compact older urban areas around the country, a trend that reduces energy consumption and carbon emissions as a side effect. In focusing less on material accumulation and more on qualitative experience in daily life, post-materialists unintentionally do the environment a favor.

Post-materialist impacts on the global environment turn out to be more than unintentional. We will now empirically tie down the link between post-materialism and direct support for environmental protection and climate stabilization. What do researchers know about the relationship between post-materialist values and concern for the environment and climate change, and how do they know what they know?

Social scientists investigate relationships between demographic, environmental, and attitudinal variables using a range of survey research and statistical techniques. In studies of human values and the environment, researchers draw on large statistical samples for their basic data such as the World Values Survey, covering 50 countries and asking respondents a variety of questions about their lives and personal attitudes and beliefs, or the International Social Survey program's 2000 module on the Environment conducted in 26 countries on topics related to environmental concern. A commonly applied approach for sorting out relationships among variables is regression analysis, a procedure that determines whether a dependent variable is affected statistically by hypothesized independent variables. Surveys, for example, ask respondents about the degree of their concern about climate change, or their willingness to pay more taxes to improve environmental quality, and the extent to which they hold post-materialist and other sorts of values or beliefs. Researchers apply regression analysis to the results of such surveys and test whether respondent environmental concern is statistically affected by post-materialist values, various other attitudes, and demographic characteristics such as age and income. In this way, the effect of post-materialism on environmental concern can be estimated holding other independent variables constant.

Richard Englehart, the leading chronicler of the global trend to post-material values, published a paper back in 1995 suggesting that post-materialists express greater support for environmental protection than others. To make his case, he used simple bar graphs of survey data on post-material values and support for the environment without engaging in extensive statistical tests.[1] Since then, a number of more detailed statistical studies confirm the positive connection between individual environmental concern and post-materialism.[2] This is the case both for general expressions of

---

[1]Inglehart, "Public Support for Environmental Protection: Objective Problems and Subjective Values in 43 Societies."

environmental concern and more specific worries about climate change, as well expressions in the form of willingness to pay added taxes for funding environmental improvement or reducing climate change. Post-materialists above all support human self-expression and individual freedom, but they also want a quality global environment.

While post-materialism is important, researchers find evidence for other determinants of environmental concern as well, such as how it is positively affected by educational attainment and specific knowledge about the environment. Not just values but knowledge matters, both in the form of general educational achievement and a detailed awareness of environmental issues. Beyond these, being a women or relatively young results in more intense expressions of environmental concern, although one study finds environmental concern to be greatest for middle-aged respondents. Similarly, personal actions to improve the environment, such as recycling or green political action, intensifies environmental concern just as does a liberal political orientation. In countries at earlier stages of economic development, conservatives and liberals surprisingly both express strong concern about environmental degradation, but as an economy matures and becomes more capitalist, and as the most serious environmental problems are addressed in response to political pressure from a growing middle class, conservatives lose their worries about the environment and become rigorously oriented to economic expansion as a primary social goal, environment be damned.[3] This is quite an amazing result about the

---

[2]John Gelissen, "Explaining Popular Support for Environmental Protection: A Multilevel Analysis of 50 Nations," *Environment and Behavior* 39, no. 3 (2007).

[3]See the following references for the details behind the statistical results described here: Ibid.; A. Franzen and R. Meyer, "Environmental Attitudes in Cross-National Perspective: A Multilevel Analysis of the ISSP 1993 and 2000," *European Sociological Review* 26, no. 2 (2009); J. E. Givens and A. K. Jorgenson, "The Effects of Affluence, Economic Development, and Environmental Degradation on Environmental Concern: A Multilevel Analysis," *Organization & Environment* 24, no. 1 (2011); Raphael Nawrotzki, "The Politics of Environmental Concern: A Cross-National Analysis," *Organization & Environment* 25(2012); Berit Kvaloy, Henning Finseraas, and Ola Listhaug, "The Publics' Concern for Global Warming: A Cross-National Study of 47 Countries," *Journal of Peace Research* 49(2012); Kvaloy, Finseraas, and Listhaug, "The Publics' Concern for Global Warming: A Cross-National Study of 47 Countries."; E. Tjernstrom and T. Tietenberg, "Do Differences in Attitudes Explain Differences in National Climate Change Policies?," *Ecological Economics* 65(2012).

environment and politics suggesting that liberals and conservatives find common ground in the right circumstances. But once an economy achieves a threshold of affluence and a modicum of control over the most gregarious pollution problems, business coalitions against environmental regulation form to retard environmental improvement in favor of unhindered economic expansion, a phenomenon very apparent in the U.S. over the last fifty years. Here liberals and conservatives part company. American political conservatives today are among the staunchest climate change deniers and liberals the most intense believers, except of course for scientists who have the highest belief level of all. To summarize our findings so far, concern for the environment depends positively on post-materialist values, education, being young, being a woman, specific knowledge of the issue, and a liberal political orientation.

Climate change as a problem possesses features that sharply distinguish it from other environmental issues. Unlike air pollution in the form of smoke or ground level ozone or water pollution in lakes and rivers, the effects of climate change lack direct visibility. We can't see carbon emissions, and we can't trace natural disasters such as Hurricane Katrina directly and unambiguously to climatic warming. Climate change, as real as it is, remains an abstract hypothesis and requires special science-based knowledge to be understood. Affluent countries such as the United States have made substantial progress in addressing visible pollution, but not so much for climatic warming. Unlike most other pollution problems, climate change is global in scope and results from greenhouse gas emissions no matter where they occur. The contribution of any but the largest and wealthiest countries to greenhouse gas emissions is such a small part of the total, that individual actions by most countries to curtail emissions would have little impact on the problem as a whole. In the absence of a globally coordinated approach to limiting greenhouse gases, no single country has much incentive to do anything about the problem. Climate change thus requires combined action by all countries for real effectiveness, a deeply challenging prospect.

Nonetheless, apart from the U.S. and a few other high-emission countries, modest progress has been made in addressing climate change through the 1997 Kyoto Protocol. Countries to jump on the

Kyoto bandwagon first with an early treaty approval possessed certain features: Already relatively high ratios of Gross Domestic Product (GDP) to energy consumed and low rates of greenhouse emissions per capita; relatively high levels of educational achievement; well developed democratic institutions; and a record of cooperation with other countries on global issues.[4] One would expect less of a challenge for countries in meeting Kyoto emissions reduction targets if they already possessed high rates of energy efficiency per unit of GDP and if they already had relatively low levels of CO_2 emissions per capita, and countries with these two features were indeed predominant among the early approvers of the Kyoto Protocol. One would also expect that a national commitment to education and political democracy would matter as well for early Kyoto approval as would the possession of a "universalist" orientation to global cooperation. In contrast to early approvers, the U.S., with its extraordinary levels of per capita fossil fuel energy consumption, faced greater costs than many countries in reducing emissions. Substantial political opposition to the Kyoto Protocol in Congress by the fossil fuel lobby and business interests led to its defeat in the treaty approval process. Without the approval of the Kyoto Protocol by the U.S., the European Union became the backbone of the treaty among the world's largest greenhouse gas emitters. The original fifteen EU member nations unanimously approved the treaty and collectively adopted centrally regulated greenhouse gas emissions reductions and tradable emission allowances.

A post-Kyoto Protocol survey in the EU shows strong citizen support for their region-wide system of environmental regulation, especially among the original fifteen member-states. As in many studies of environmental attitudes, the degree of post-materialist values held by EU respondents positively affects their willingness to sacrifice income for the environment. Also, as is typically found in other studies, younger EU respondents and political liberals lend greater support than others to spending money on environmental improvement. A positive impact of GDP per capita on willingness

---

[4]Sammy Zahran et al., "Ecological Development and Global Climate Change: A Cross-National Study of Kyoto Protocol Ratification," *Society & Natural Resources* 20, no. 1 (2007).

to pay for environmental improvement across all countries of the EU supports the idea that more income leads to a greater demand for environmental quality and an enlarged capacity to pay for it.[5] As one would expect, citizens of less-wealthy Eastern European member nations that joined the EU later express a lesser degree of support for EU environmental regulation.[6] To sum up, post-materialism, youth, education, and economic prosperity matter for support of environmental improvement in the EU.

These results for the EU do not mean that worries about the environment and climate change are confined to just the affluent countries of the world. A recent study of 47 countries, including both rich and poor, using the latest World Values Survey finds the following: Concern about global warming is unchanging across countries with higher and lower GDP and CO_2 emissions per capita; concern is positively affected by post-materialism, a leftwing political orientation, religious involvement, and education level; concern is negatively affected by being a male respondent, having a rightwing political orientation, and experiencing weather-related natural disasters; and middle-aged respondents express greater concern for global warming than either older or younger ones.[7]

None of these relationships is too surprising except for the negative effect of weather-related natural disasters. Disasters cause a decrease in concern about climate change among respondents, contrary to expectations. One would think that exposure to a climate related disaster would increase respondent climate concerns, but for many the link between weather and climate change may not be well understood. As a practical matter, those recently affected by such disasters may have immediate problems that push climate change down their list of worries. Figuring out

---

[5]For the role of income in expressions of environmental concern, see Axel Franzen and Dominikus Vogl, "Acquiescence and the Willingness to Pay for Environmental Protection: A Comparison of the ISSP, WVS, and EVS," *Social Science Quarterly* 94, no. 3, (2012), 657-639; Jurgen Gerhards and Holger Lengfeld, "Support for European Union Environmental Policy by Citizens of EU-Member and Accession States," *Comparative Sociology* 7(2008).
[6]Gerhards and Lengfeld, "Support for European Union Environmental Policy by Citizens of EU-Member and Accession States."
[7]Kvaloy, Finseraas, and Listhaug, "The Publics' Concern for Global Warming: A Cross-National Study of 47 Countries."

how to recover from a flood today for many no doubt takes precedence over concerns with the uncertain future effects of climate change.

The lack of a positive relationship between concern for climate change and income across rich and poor countries together makes more sense for a global problem such as climate change than it does for a local problem such as ozone pollution. At a local level, prosperity brings with it greater demands for improvements in environmental quality, as noted above. At a global level, low-income countries will bear the brunt of climate change costs in the form of drought or flooding, and it is the high-income countries of the world that possess most responsibility for future climatic warming. Given this reality, equal concern about climate change between low- and high-income countries looks less surprising. Wealthy nations may well face a demand for climate stabilization related to income, but it is the poor of the world that will experience the full force of climate change damage. The poor of the world face the indignity of a problem foisted on them by the rich, and it is the rich that have the primary responsibly for cleaning it up. If anything in these circumstances, the world's poor should be expressing more concern about climate change than the rich, and we will now see that in at least one survey they do.

Two economists recently used the International Social Survey program's 26-country 2000 module on the environment to tease out the effects of respondent attitudes and other factors on the perceived seriousness of global warming and the ultimate impact of such perceptions on actual greenhouse gas emissions.[8] What drives climate concerns among citizens, and do such concerns matter for government actions on climate change? Based on a large sample of individuals in the 26 countries, the researchers find the perceived seriousness of greenhouse warming to be influenced at statistically significant levels as follows: Positively by respondent affinity for the global community and support for public goods in general and long-term public goods in particular (such as climatic stability); positively by educational attainment, liberal political affiliation, and urban residency; and negatively by a lack of

---

[8]Tjernstrom and Tietenberg, "Do Differences in Attitudes Explain Differences in National Climate Change Policies?."

familiarity with the climate change issue, respondent age, and per capita income.

In earlier chapters we talked about "universalist" values that include a general concern for the well being of humanity as a whole and for the natural environment in general, and we noted that post-materialists tend to be universalists. The statistical results just summarized suggest that universalist values in the form of global affinity, support for public goods, and a liberal political orientation positively impact the perceived seriousness of climate change. This infers that post-materialism would have a similar impact were it included in the study since post-materialists tend to be universalists. Because of its lack of direct visibility, knowledge of the climate change issue matters for judging its seriousness, and the statistical evidence in this study indicates this to be the case. Finally, the impact of income on the perceived threat of climate change is negative, supporting the idea that low-income respondents express greater climate concern because they are the ones who bear relatively greater harm from the problem and less responsibility for it.

A huge challenge for all of us globally is to bring climate change to a halt and temperatures back to levels that no longer pose a threat to life on earth. The philosophy we possess affects the values we have, and our task here is to set out how in practice values matter for what we do in the world. We now know that post-materialist and universalist values along with lower per capita national income, greater educational attainment, and a liberal political outlook make a difference globally in beliefs about the seriousness of climate change. The question to be addressed is simple: Do such beliefs matter for climate change itself? Let's take a look at research on just this question.

Countries with relatively low actual growth of greenhouse gas emissions possess the following: A more extensive belief among their citizens that climate change is a serious issue; a greater degree of press freedom; greater citizen trust of government information on pollution; and the absence of either very high or very low per capita GDP levels relative to the average.[9] What do these research results mean for the impact of philosophy and

---

[9]Ibid.

values on real world actions? In a democracy responsive to citizen concerns, we would expect worries about climate change to be reflected in government actions to limit greenhouse gases, and the findings tell us that they do. The greater the proportion of citizens in a country who believe that greenhouse warming is dangerous for the environment, the lower the pace of growth in greenhouse gas emissions, inferring that governments must be taking action to limit emissions. The curtailing of such emissions is augmented by press freedom, which brings greater awareness to the public about issues of importance such as climate change, and by public trust in government information about the environment. Finally, whether a country is wealthy or poor doesn't play a role in the determination of actual practice for limiting greenhouse gas emissions, suggesting that cross-country income differences operate through citizen concern about the environment and not apart from it. As already noted, individual citizen worries about climate change are negatively affected by income.

The essential take away message here is that citizen attitudes matter in limiting greenhouse gas emissions. With a rising proportion of post-materialists in the global population who favor doing something about climate change, actual results look to be on the horizon. Countries whose citizens express concern about climate change have done more than others historically to limit their greenhouse emission growth. The question remains whether post-materialist political influence will be strong enough in the future to fully offset the incredible power of vested fossil fuel economic and political interests, especially in the United States. To this issue we now turn.

***

U.S. environmental survey respondents have the special distinction of expressing a below average concern with climate change, a below average knowledge of the subject, and a below average trust in government information on the environment.[10] These survey findings help to explain why the U.S. in the last two decades failed to sign onto the Kyoto Protocol and adopt regulatory limitations on greenhouse gas emissions.

---

[10]Ibid.

An environmentalist transported by a time machine from the late 1960s and early 1970s to the present day would be surprised and shocked by a lack of U.S. action on climate change. With the election of President Obama in 2008, expectations were high that Congress would past a cap and trade bill placing limits on overall greenhouse gas emissions. A proposed bill was to accomplish this through a system of emission allowances that would shrink in number slowly over a thirty-five year period. These allowances were to be bought and sold in a market that would permit emitters with high control costs to buy allowances from those with low costs, reducing the economic burden of forestalling climate change. The House of Representatives passed such a bill, but the Senate never approved it.

To the President's credit, his administration has dramatically tightened future fuel efficiency standards for motor vehicles that bite deeply into carbon emissions, invested government funds in clean energy businesses, offered subsidies for investments in carbon-free energy production, and started the process of regulating greenhouse gases from utilities and industry under the Clean Air Act. In the meantime, industry interests and conservative groups have mounted a substantial lobbying and public relations campaign against greenhouse gas regulation, including attempts to discredit scientific studies on the relationship between burning fossil fuels and climate warming, an effort that seems to have paid off by suppressing public climate change worries.

Environmental politics differed substantially back in the early 1970s when such legislative landmarks as the Clean Air Act, Clean Water Act, and Endangered Species Act were passed by Congress and signed into law by a Republican President, Richard M. Nixon. In those days, environmental issues ranked high in public concern, and the environmental movement looked invincible. Industry lobbyists seemed impotent in the face of a well-organized and popular effort to mitigate a variety of harms to the country's natural environment. The success of environmentalism began its long decline with a series of economic crises in the mid-1970s and early 1980s initiated by the 1973 Arab oil embargo undertaken to punish the U.S. for its support of Israel in the Yon Kippur War. Even though the embargo ended, world oil prices continued a dramatic rise with the creation of the OPEC oil cartel and its success at limiting world oil supplies. This turn of events caused global economic havoc including runaway inflation and a double-dip recession in the U.S. Such deeply serious economic problems served to strengthen opposition to environmental regulation and enabled business interests to mount a successful campaign of opposition both in the courts and Congress against implementation of environmental legislation by the Environmental Protection Agency. Life for the environmental movement toughened further with a conservative turn in national politics ushered in by the ascendency of Ronald Reagan to the presidency in 1980.

It was not until the passage of the 1990 Clean Air Act Amendments in the first Bush administration that the environmental movement experienced any success at all in the legislative arena. The 1990 Amendments created a cap and trade system for sulfur dioxide emissions implicated in the problem of acid rain seriously damaging pristine lakes and forests in the northeastern U.S. Although the 1990 Amendments were successfully implemented at below expected costs to the public, the U.S. environmental movement has achieved little since, especially in bringing greenhouse gases under control. This has happened despite accumulating scientific evidence of the link between greenhouse emissions and climatic warming and growing evidence of already accruing climate-change harms.[11]

While both the U.S. and Europe exhibit comparable trends in the growth of post-materialist values, European environmental concerns and actions on limiting climate change outpace those in the U.S. Based on the rise of post-materialism, the U.S. and Europe should have similar trends in environmental concerns and accomplishments, but they don't, at least in the last two decades. Because of its greater energy intensity brought on by a more spatially expansive and auto-oriented way of life, the fossil fuel industry is relatively larger in this country than Europe, and fossil fuels constitute a powerful economic interest with a well-honed political capacity to oppose greenhouse gas emissions regulation. The motor vehicle industry once was in the same political boat as fossil fuels, but this is less the case now with the necessity of the

---

[11]Douglas E. Booth, *Hooked on Growth: Economic Addictions and the Environment* (Lanham: Rowman & Littlefield, 2004). See Chapter 8.

recent federal bailout to save the industry from extinction. Hardly a peep arose from the auto industry with the imposition of increased fuel efficiency standards by the Obama administration.

Despite environmentalism's political setbacks in the U.S., there is room for hope in the future. The continuation of the post-materialist trend will slowly but inexorably raise the average level public concern for both the local and global environment if past behavior as documented by researchers holds true. Post-materialists will also continue to adopt a more compact, energy-efficient form of urban life that will serve as a drag on fossil fuel demand. Finally, there are good reasons for governments to impose a price on greenhouse emissions, either through an emissions tax or a cap and trade system, as we will now explain. Philosophy will matter in the form of a trend to post-materialism, but economic trends will matter as well in the curtailing of fossil fuel consumption and greenhouse gas emissions.

***

Let's begin with the short story on the economics of clean energy, solar and wind especially, and energy conservation. (For the long story, see my *The Coming Good Boom*).[12] Energy conservation, the simple act of using less, turns out to be a "free lunch" in the eyes of most experts. Over the next forty years, we can reduce our consumption of energy per capita by about a third at zero net cost. This means that cost savings pay for the investment required to achieve a third less energy consumption through such measures as buying hybrids and other fuel efficient motor vehicles, adding insulation to our attics, installing energy efficient lighting, living in more compact and energy efficient buildings, and expanding mass transit systems.

On top of efficiency gains, to get unhooked from carbon-based energy, we will still have to come up with the other two thirds of our current energy consumption, and if we want to bring climate change to a screeching halt, this will have to be from zero greenhouse emission sources such as wind, solar, biofuels, and nuclear. Because of public opposition, expanding nuclear power beyond current levels can probably be ruled out, leaving us with

---

[12]Booth, *The Coming Good Boom: Creating Prosperity for All and Saving the Environment through Compact Living*, especially Chapters 8 and 9.

wind, solar, biofuels and a variety of sources with a smaller potential such as geothermal and various kinds of waterpower including small scale hydro and tidal.[13] Biofuels, such as ethanol from corn, haven't been very promising so far because energy inputs into their production exceed the energy available in the output. The future does look brighter for biofuel from agriculture and other kinds of waste with progress being made on the technology of converting plant materials containing cellulose to ethanol and garbage to hydrogen. Assuming an energy system based on solar and wind, in forty years our inflation adjusted energy bill might be 10-15 percent higher than it is today, but since our real incomes are likely to rise much more than this because of labor productivity gains (each of us producing more stuff), the relative energy bill burden will actually decline.[14] Wind is already closing in the on the current cost of energy from coal, and solar will do the same within the next twenty years according to Energy Department projections.

Such cost reductions have as their source a standard economic phenomenon—the more you produce of something, the lower its average cost. This idea of "scale economies" will make solving the problem of climate change less costly, but it also presents a critical barrier to transforming our energy system. Right now electrical generating volumes for wind and solar are insufficient to compete with coal and natural gas, but if they were scaled-up, their unit costs would fall. Fossil fuels unfairly get a free ride on the external costs they cause from global climate change damage. If a prices were imposed per ton for greenhouse gas emissions that accounted for such costs, fossil fuel prices would rise relative to clean energy and investment in wind and solar would expand, causing their unit costs to decline at an accelerated pace as scale economies kick in.

Economists suggest two alternatives for getting climate change costs incorporated into fossil fuel prices: a tax on emissions or a cap and trade system. Either one places a price on greenhouse gas emissions that fossil fuel producers must pay. The scientific

---

[13]Nuclear currently supplies 8 percent of total energy consumed in the U.S. See U.S. Energy Information Administration, "Annual Energy Review 2011," U.S. Energy Information Administration, www.eia.gov/totalenergy/data/annual/pdf/sec2.pdf.
[14]A 1% annual increase in output per capita over 40 years would mean a 50% increase in incomes on average.

clearinghouse for climate change research, the Intergovernmental Panel on Climate Change (IPCC), suggests that a $100 per metric ton global price on carbon emissions (and their equivalents in terms of climate change potential) will be needed by 2030 to put a lid on climatic warming. Assuming that such a cost is fully passed onto the consumer, the result would be about a dollar increase in the price per gallon of gasoline and a $.10 increase per kilowatt of electrical energy generated from coal. Such increases would cause coal to be much more expensive as a source of electrical energy than either wind or solar, and give a boost to biofuel and electric powered motor vehicles. If the $100 price increase per ton of emissions were spread out over 15 years, this would amount to less than a penny increase per kilowatt of coal-fired electricity and $.07 increase per gallon of gas annually. Everyone would have plenty of time to adjust to energy price increases by shifting to wind and solar power, more energy efficient housing and appliances, and high-mileage motor vehicles that run on clean energy. Because the current boom in natural gas has driven the cost of gas-powered electricity generation below coal-fired plants, the life of carbon-based energy will be extended under a carbon pricing regime, but since the carbon content of natural gas per unit energy is only about half that of coal, greenhouse emissions will still be reduced. Eventually carbon-free energy will be cheaper than even natural gas according to Energy Department projections as the price of carbon emissions rise over time.

In comparing the virtues of cap trade to a carbon tax, there isn't really much to argue about. A carbon tax of $100 would directly fix the price of emitting a ton of carbon, and the volume of emissions would be determined by the decisions of energy consumers. The basic idea is that consumers would reduce their use of increasingly expensive fossil fuels and expand their consumption of relatively less costly untaxed clean energy. Under cap and trade, the government would fix an annual emissions limit for each of the next forty years that would in the end drive emissions to near zero. In each year, emission allowances for the volumes allowed within the caps would be issued to emitters. These allowances could either be auctioned off by government or given away, and in either case their price would be established by market forces. Auctioning has the advantage of creating a new source of government revenue comparable to collecting a tax. Over a twenty year period the revenue collected in the U.S. could amount as much as $4 trillion and could be used to put a substantial dent in our national debt currently running around $16 trillion. If the $100 price by 2030 is enough to do the work of capping global warming, then a tax and cap and trade are essentially equivalent. In the first instance, government sets the price per ton of carbon and in the second it sets the volume of emissions allowed. The tax is conceptually simpler, but allowances assure that emissions caps are realized and give industries more flexibility in meeting their limits. Personally, I am agnostic on the two approaches; either will do the trick.

An attractive feature in the current political climate for putting a price on greenhouse emissions is its revenue generating potential to use in reducing the national debt in a manner that increases the burden on consumers very slowly. Even more attractive is the ability for consumers to avoid much of the government-created price on carbon through improving their personal energy efficiency and by switching to clean energy sources, something that would be infeasible if government debt were instead paid down through higher taxes on incomes tough to avoid.

A second attractive feature of a greenhouse emissions price is its potential for stimulating an economic boom based on the creation of a new clean energy industry. An essential economic virtue of clean energy is its ability to generate employment. Both wind and solar require a wide range of employee skills for design, installation, maintenance, and operations, and the volume of employment needed per unit of energy is much higher for solar and wind energy than it is for fossil fuels. Studies estimate that the production of electricity from either coal or natural gas requires an average of 0.11 person years of labor per gigawatt hour of power, while solar photovoltaics use and average of 0.87 person years and wind 0.17 person years per gigawatt hour.[15] These numbers are calculated over the typical lifespan of energy production facilities and account for labor employed in design, installation,

---

[15]Max Wei, Shana Patadia, and Daniel M. Kammen, "Putting Renewables and Energy Efficiency to Work: How Many Jobs can the Clean Energy Industry Generate in the U.S.?," *Energy Policy* 38(2010).

maintenance, and operations. Clearly, clean energy is much more labor intensive than fossil fuels, and converting energy supply from fossil fuels to clean energy will add jobs to the economy. The same is the case for reducing energy consumption through energy efficiency measures adding about .38 person years to employment per gigawatt hour of energy saved. A study summarizing these findings suggests that meeting growth in energy demand completely from energy efficiency measures combined with 30 percent of electrical energy coming from clean sources in 2030 will add 4 million jobs per year to the economy net of reductions in fossil fuels. Scaling this up to a totally green energy electrical economy, would multiply this number to more than 12 million jobs. Right now 60 percent of energy consumed occurs outside of the electricity sector in motor vehicle and other types of transportation, dwellings, industries, commercial establishments, and agriculture.[16] In a clean energy economy, an expanding share of total energy consumed will come from electricity as opposed to solid or liquid fuels, meaning that net employment gains by 2050 will be even more than our projected 12 million jobs. Liquid fuels from biomass will require about twice as much employment per unit energy as natural gas, suggesting that even if we stick to liquid fuels for powering our transportation system, clean fuels will stimulate more jobs on net than the fossil fuels they replace. Besides biofuels, a second potential huge gaseous fuel source is hydrogen produced from electricity, stimulating a further expansion in electricity sector employment. Hydrogen in turn can be used to power fuel cells in motor vehicles and elsewhere that provide a mobile and flexible source of electrical energy.

Placing a price on carbon will have the immediate impact of telling everyone that the days of fossil fuels are numbered, and that money is to be made instead in clean energy. This will spark an immediate boom in the design and installation of clean energy capacity and a front-loading of employment in solar, wind, and biofuels. There will be some employment leakage to imports, as has been the case recently for low-end solar panels, but the research and design as well as installation portion of employment will be predominantly a local affair and will constitute most of the

---

[16]Ibid.

jobs created in solar energy. Given the scale and bulk of wind generating equipment, manufacture and assembly will normally take place close to the site, and the same will be the case for large-scale thermal solar facilities springing up in desert landscapes in the U.S. and elsewhere. Biofuels production will be tied to the waste sources they depend on. A surge in clean energy will be accompanied by added employment growth in energy conservation work as well, such as upgrading heating and lighting systems and insulating older residences and commercial buildings. With rising fuel costs, the construction of energy efficient light rail lines will look increasingly attractive as an alternative to the automobile for getting around. Light rail expansion will also have the side benefit of accelerating the trend to living compactly by increasing the ease of residing in high density, walkable neighborhoods near transit lines. Taxes are normally thought of as a depressant to economic expansion, but a tax on greenhouse emissions will set off an economic boom driven by clean energy. This boom will in turn create diverse new employment opportunities across a wide range of skills helping to resolve challenging unemployment problems, especially in older, denser cities suited to xenergy efficient living.

Politicians in the future will have increasing difficulty ignoring the growing clout of politically active post-materialists who will be an expanding share of the voting population and who already express deep concern about climate change and environmental decline. A greenhouse gas emissions tax will gain in political popularity, not only as a virtuous environmental and boom-creating economic measure, but also as one with the special side benefit of raising tax revenues over the long haul and bringing down the level of government debt. What could be better? Once these virtues of clean energy are fully recognized, the power of the currently formidable fossil fuel lobby will look much less imposing. Philosophy in the form of a growing post-materialism will turn out to matter along with the virtues of clean energy economics in finding our path to a better future.

9 The Experience Economy

In a strictly biological conception of economic behavior, mental experience drives material acquisitions. A feeling of hunger pushes us to acquire and consume food; cold temperatures, wind, and rain stimulate us to gain protective clothing or cover; sexual and family love cause us to copulate, reproduce, and acquire the material requirements for nurturing, protecting, and defending our lovers and kin. Mental motivations combined with the contingencies of daily experience drive our accumulation of material goods essential for long-term survival.

We humans in contrast to other species enjoy the privilege of ecological release, meaning that we needn't spend every waking hour in the satisfaction of our material necessities.[1] This privilege comes to us by virtue of our special mental faculties that permit us to exploit nature's resources at uniquely high rates of economic efficiency. As a consequence, we can of course engage in the production of material goods well beyond our basic needs, or we can sit around and contemplate the beauties of the world around us, sing songs, or think the big thoughts. We can produce more than we need and use it to pay others to entertain us with stories or dance, teach us how to do mathematics, or to take us on guided nature walks. Economics doesn't distinguish between baking bread and presenting Shakespeare's Richard the III; both are economic goods for which people are willing to pay, and both offer mental stimuli and satisfaction. There is an important difference between them, however; bread is enjoyed in an act of physical consumption, and the pleasure of Richard the III is a perceptual and mental experience. The loaf of sourdough French bread I gobble down becomes unavailable to you, but we can both experience Shakespeare together without detracting from each other's pleasure. The experience of consuming a loaf of bread involves a using up of a material good, and the experience of consuming Richard the III doesn't. Experience requires stimulus from the physical world, but not necessarily a substantial physical transformation of that world. Experiences can be placed on a

---

[1]Marshall Sahlins, *Stone Age Economics* (London: Tavistock, 1974).

spectrum, heavily dependent on altering the material world at one end (eating bread and drinking wine), and not requiring any alteration at all on the other (enjoying a sunset). At one end you and I cannot consume the same exact material thing (a particular glass of wine), and at the other we can (the sunset).

Complications arise. We can share a Shakespeare play, but if the audience is too big, some of us won't be able to get close enough to perceive all the action on the stage. In sharing a physical phenomenon, crowding can be a problem. Too many people detract from the experience. In some cases, such as a rock concert, where audience reaction is part of the experience, too few people instead can be a problem. In wilderness hiking, where the act of it does little to modify the physical world, the sharing of it can detract from the experience if one is running into someone on the trail too often or if all the good campsites are taken. In short, the number of people sharing an otherwise benign experience (i.e. with an innocuous physical impact) matters. In some case the more the merrier, and in some more is bad.[2]

We will need some language here to distinguish benign from physically degrading experiences. Let's call the later "entropic" experiences—they degrade the physical environment in some way, reducing it to a less organized state—and let's stick to "benign" for those that don't.[3] We also need a clarification. While the direct enjoyment of a Shakespeare play is benign, its production is not. The stage, the costumes, and all the other necessary paraphernalia of making a play happen re-arranges the physical world just as does the making of a loaf of bread. The difference between the two goods is that consuming the play is benign and the bread entropic. You and I can't consume the same loaf of bread but we can the same play. Some things in life are actually entropically free—you and I can enjoy the same sunset and the physical world is unchanged from what it otherwise would be. Of course, if the sunset is over Sonoran desert mountains, you and I will have used up material resources in our travels and caused some physical entropy, but once on the scene the extra physical changes we cause

---

[2]Mancur Olson, *The Logic of Collective Action: Public Goods and the Theory of Groups* (Cambridge: Harvard University Press, 1965).
[3]For economic application of the idea of entropy, see Herman Daly, E., *Steady-State Economics*, ed. 2nd (Washington D.C.: Island Press, 1991).

in watching the sunset becomes vanishingly small. Of course just walking around the desert will have some impact, but not much, especially if we step with care.

Around the globalized economy of today entropic consumption continues to be a really big deal. In the affluent countries of the world, what many of us want is the experience of more and new and novel material possessions. We want big houses with big yards and lots of cool furniture, powerful and sleek looking cars, lots of high tech gadgets and entertainment systems, nice clothes, and great cuisine. In producing, acquiring, and using such goods, we massively rearrange the physical world. The resulting experience of enjoying all this stuff is heavily entropic, rendering us economic materialists through and through.

***

While entropic consumption and experience still rule the economic roost, physically benign experiences[4] have always been with us and seem to be gaining in popularity along with the move to post-material values. We see this in the resurgence of downtown living making easier shared activities—concerts, plays, art exhibitions, people watching in parks, squares, and sidewalk cafes, urban bike rides, using public transit, searching for reading materials in public libraries or bookstores, and watching or playing soccer or baseball. Compact urban living greases the skids of encounters with others for shared experiences. Suburban living instead facilitates spread out, low density, entropic consumption in suburban housing, shopping malls, and on the highways. A shift from the latter to the former facilitates a move from highly entropic to more benign forms of living.

Some shared experiences inadvertently occur in the normal course of daily life in cities. Moving from point A to B means a sharing of a sidewalk, a tram or bus, a bike lane, or a roadway. Moving about puts us in sensual contact with other people, buildings, public spaces, landscapes, and traffic, and our method of doing so shapes our sense experience. Riding a bike is different than driving, walking, or taking a bus. Each has its exhilarations,

---

[4]In practice, experiences lay on a spectrum from heavily entropic to completely benign (causing near-zero entropy). Here we will use the term entropic to refer to those towards the heavy end of the spectrum and benign those towards the zero end.

pleasures, pains, and frustrations. Driving can be a pleasure without traffic and with scenic views, but on a traffic-congested street, highway, or expressway, it can be tedious and stressful. The later kind of experience can be avoided in a dense, walkable, bike friendly, public transit oriented city, but less easily in a spatially expansive suburb. Some shared experiences are more consciously selected, such as hanging out on a park bench or at a sidewalk cafe or espresso shop, strolling through a museum or art gallery, sitting in a library, attending a concert or play, running or biking on a recreation path, or watching or participating in a softball game at a local play field.

Shared experiences in public settings tend to be low entropy, low cost affairs where adding one more person to the sharing pool requires little in the way of added economic resources and brings little or no harm to others. The exception occurs where such an addition leads to overcrowding or congestion, detracting from the quality of the shared experience. This would be the case for driving when an added car slows traffic, or attending a crowded public concert where one can't see the stage or an added police presence is needed to maintaining public order. The quality of some shared activities actually depend positively on the size and density of the sharing pool as Jane Jacobs tells us.[5] Sitting on a park bench with nobody walking by isn't much fun; nor is strolling down a street without other people, or sitting in an empty cafe, or going to a ball game in a half-empty stadium.

A critical virtue of densely packed cities is the variety of shared experiences close at hand in comparison to the suburbs. In the suburbs, varieties of such experiences are available, but to get to them one must drive, an energetically costly activity. Suburbs specialize more in private experiences requiring a privately owned capital stock, such as large backyards for outdoor activities, large homes filled with household amenities for indoor recreation and entertainment, and multiple motor vehicles for tooling about the countryside. In densely packed cities, outdoor and indoor recreation and entertainment is more frequently found in shared public places, and fewer private motor vehicles are needed for moving about. A substantial public capital stock is required in

---

[5] Jane Jacobs, *The Death and Life of Great American Cities* (New York: Vintage, 1961).

these places in support of a shared livability, but its wear and tear is more a function of time than of use. In suburbs by contrast, the capital stock required, with the exception of schools and roads, veers towards the private—big houses and yards, parking lots, and shopping malls.

The energy efficiency of low entropy compact urban living is well established. One might not think it off hand, but the compact cities of the world—New York, Paris, and Cairo—are among the most energy efficient, low entropy places to live.[6] Fossil fuel energy doesn't go away as you burn it up, but it is rendered into highly dispersed waste heat. This is the essence of entropy. Burn a gallon of gas or eat a French baguette, and entropy increases. In central cities as opposed to suburbs, per capita gasoline consumption and motor vehicle related carbon emissions are substantially less. The same is the case for electricity and household heating fuel consumption and their associated carbon emissions. In central city apartments, one lives in less space and shares walls and roofs reducing building surface exposure and the rate of heat or cooling loss per unit area as opposed to spatially expansive suburbs with more spacious houses and much bigger heating or cooling requirements.[7] In densely packed central cities one shares public transit and streets and sidewalks for biking and walking to a much greater extent than in the suburbs where the predominant mode of sharing is of roadways for energy intensive, privately occupied automobiles. Even if one lives in the central city and continues to drive, getting around involves shorter trips and less fuel consumption than living in the suburbs. Whatever else one does, by choosing to live in a compact central city, one reduces the entropy associated with life's daily experiences.

***

The 1950s teenage male dream when I was growing up in Seattle, Washington was obtaining a drivers license and buying a car at age 16. And it wasn't just any car, but one that was souped-

---

[6]J.R. Kenworthy, "Transport Energy Use and Greenhouse Gases in Urban Passenger Transport Systems: A Study of 84 Global Cities," (Murdoch, Western Australia: Murdoch University, 2003); Peter Newman and Jeffrey R. Kenworthy, *Sustainability and Cities: Overcoming Automobile Dependency* (Washington D.C.: Island Press, 1999).
[7]Douglas E. Booth, *The Coming Good Boom: Creating Prosperity for All and Saving the Environment through Compact Living* (Charleston: Create Space, 2010).

up, lowered, loud, and possessed of metallic paint and pin striping. For this I saved checks as a grocery store bag boy for two years. This dream today would seem quaint and definitely unfashionable. I suspect most teenage boys now would rather have a top-of-the line iPhone or gaming devise instead of a driver's license or car. In my day socializing took place in and around motor vehicles, and involved cruising around, racing, and hanging out in fast food parking lots. The leisure experience was highly entropic, burning up huge volumes of dirt-cheap gasoline. In Seattle, we couldn't wait for the newly constructed freeway system to open up so we could drive at 60 mph or better from one end of the city to the other. Now, I suspect, a high-speed Internet connection is way more important for teenagers than driving around on freeways or anywhere else.

This impression finds support in statistics on drivers' licenses and driving for young people. The average annual miles driven by Americans in this country peaked in 2004 at a little more than 10,000, and dropped 6% by 2011. The American love affair with the automobile appears to be on the wane, and post-materialist Millennials are leading the way. Between 2001 and 2009, the average yearly miles travelled by car for young people (age 16-34) decrease from 10,300 to 7,900, a drop of 23%. Over this same period, the number of 20-34 year olds without drivers' licenses increased from 10 to 15 percent.[8] A downward trend in driving could well be a consequence of dire economic conditions created by the Great Recession of 2007-2009, but the reduction began before the recession hit, and so far driving has failed to pick up in the recovery. The driving decrease is no doubt partly fed by higher real gasoline prices that will likely persist in the long run, and also by a budgetary squeeze on Millennials caused in part by rising college debt levels.[9]

Reductions in driving by young people may well originate instead in fundamental shifts in attitudes. After World War II, Americans bought into the dream of owning a single-family home in the spatially expansive and auto-dependent suburbs. People

---

[8] Elisabeth Rosenthal, "The End of Car Culture," *New York Times*, June 29, 2013.
[9] Steven E. Polzin, Xuehao Chu, and Jodi Godrey, "The Impact of Millennials' Travel Behavior on Future Personal Vehicle Travel," *Energy Strategy Reviews* http.//dx.doi.org/10.1016/j.esr.2014.10.003(2014).

wanted to drive and were perfectly happy with the necessity of a motor vehicle for getting from point A to B. For Millennials, the bloom is off the auto-oriented suburban rose, and they now look more often to densely packed, transit-oriented central cities as places to live. Recent surveys tell us that young people more than other age groups claim to have made conscious efforts to reduce their driving. The youngest and oldest age groups more than others prefer to live in so-called "smart growth" neighborhoods with a mix of single and multiple family dwellings and access to public transit, stores, restaurants, libraries, and schools within walking distance. The young especially prize nearby rail links and bus routes. The college-educated young and older empty nesters, as we discussed earlier, have fostered much of the four decades old boom in downtown living in many central cities previously suffering rampant population losses. To put it simply, densely packed older cities today offer access to activities and experiences less readily available in the suburbs, and in those cities getting around by walking, biking, or taking public transit is often easier than driving. One can move about readily in the city without driving much, but to live in the suburbs without a car would be a serious challenge.[10]

In my youth social interaction required a car. To see friends one drove. The car was the admission ticket to the teenage club and an essential symbol of one's standing in the social pecking order. Today social life is increasingly an online affair. Communication is virtual and immediate and doesn't require physical travel. Through texting, Facebook, Twitter, and online gaming, young people much more than others socialize virtually rather than driving to meet their friends. When they do get together, they are more inclined than their elders to walk, bike, or take public transit, all eased by living at high densities in walkable cities with bike sharing programs and decent bus and rail systems. Getting around cities is also facilitated by smartphone apps that tell you when the next bus is coming or where the nearest bike-sharing site can be found. When you absolutely need a car, you can rent

---

[10]Tony Dutzik, Jeff Inglis, and Phineas Baxandall, "Milleniansl in Motion: Changing Travel Habits of Young Americans and the Implications for Public Policy," (Boston: U.S. PIRG Education Fund, 2014).

one quickly through Zip Car or Cars to Go; ownership isn't required.[11]

Substituting virtual sociality for driving isn't an entropic free lunch. Huge energy-sucking data centers keep the Internet running and make possible all the stuff we like to do on our devices. Keeping an iPhone charged for the average user over the course of a year requires about 24 kilowatt hours (kWh) of energy, a little less than the 33 kWh used up burning a gallon of gasoline. But when you add the average annual energy use for the Internet, the per-iPhone user energy requirement rises to about 388 kWh, a little more than a kWh per day.[12] Driving 10,000 miles a year at 25 miles per gallon, however, requires a whopping 13,200 kWh. Entropically speaking, your iPhone and your car are not in the same ballpark. Substituting the Internet for driving indeed reduces energy consumption.

Not all sociality occurs online for Millennials. When they get together, they want doing so eased by close proximity. Instead of living in spread-out, auto-dependent suburbs so loved by their elders, Millennials prefer more densely packed urban centers with abundant places to meet, such as cafes and espresso shops, and the convenience of getting to them by biking or walking. The suburban dream has lost its cache for Millennials who see their aspirations best satisfied in downtown living. This could change, however, if central city education reform is slow in coming and Millennials opt for the suburbs to assure access to good schools for their kids just as their parents did.

***

The common dimension of the low-entropy experience economy is sharing. Some such shared experiences are open access (a concert in the park) and some are not (a major league baseball game); some fully cover costs from admissions (movies in theaters) and some don't (museums); and, for most, fixed costs tend to be large relative to variable costs. User ownership of material goods is normally not important to the shared experience, the one exception being the sharing of roadways that requires the

---

[11] Ibid.
[12] Bryan Walsh, "The Surprisingly Large Energy Footprint of the Digital Economy " Time Magazine, http://science.time.com/2013/08/14/power-drain-the-digital-cloud-is-using-more-energy-than-you-think/.

driver to possess a motor vehicle. In some cases, private wealth matters for enjoyment of an experience due to high admission fees—i.e. the opera, a Broadway play, or a first tier symphony orchestra. In some, status or self-expression display through privately supplied and consumed fashion is a part of the package. But for many shared experiences, public sector supply, not private, is the essential element—i.e. museums, community centers, swimming pools, stadiums, streets, sidewalks, parks, squares, and libraries.

Museums provide an interesting hybrid case for shared experience. Some are public, some are private, and most receive some public funding. Their primary dilemma comes in their cost structure. A museum's fixed costs, those that don't vary with attendance, are huge relative to their variable costs. The essential thing that museums do is display their collections that are generally costly to acquire, house, and maintain. Letting in a few more patrons to see the collection usually doesn't cost much. If museums cranked their full operating costs into their admission fees, they would price themselves out of the market—hence the need for outside contributions or public funding. Of course if you are a patron, museums unsurprisingly put a lot of effort into gaining your contributions through memberships or charitable giving. Memberships that give you free admission often look like a deal if you think you will attend more than two or three times a year and cost museums very little per visit. With free admission attendance becomes a self-fulfilling prophesy that you might avoid if you had to pay per visit. Remember, your membership generates revenues for museums at very little cost in wear and tear from your attendance. The larger attendance figures from memberships will be a plus in seeking outside funding, public or private. Because museums normally draw on a regional, a national, or even an international market, they do best located in urban centers where regional access is easiest and where hotels, restaurant, and other tourist facilities are abundant. Locals who, by virtue of close proximity, use their museums with relatively high frequency benefit from a regional and sometimes even national or international patron network that brings in funding to cover fixed costs and keep admission and membership fees in affordable bounds.

Unlike museums with most of their costs attributable to collection development and facilities, the performing arts are heavily labor intensive. Think of a symphony orchestra and all its musicians, or better yet an opera with not only performers on stage, but an orchestra in the pit and numerous stagehands behind the scenes. Such labor intensity leads to what economist William Baumol coined as the "cost disease."[13] In a capitalist economy, through investment in new plant and equipment, educational progress, and technological change, labor productivity, the hourly volume of output per worker for the economy as a whole, advances 1-2 percent a year and is normally accompanied by an equivalent growth in the average hourly real (inflation adjusted) wage. In recent decades this has not been the case so much at the lower end of the pay scale, with the owners of capital taking a larger share of the total output pie and labor a lesser share because of its diminished bargaining power caused by globalization, weakened labor unions, and labor saving technological advance. The critical problem for labor intensive performing arts organizations is this: The annual salaries they pay for their employees will need to advance by 1-2 percent a year in order to remain competitive with other skilled occupations. An orchestra today uses roughly the same technology in delivering its product as did its counterpart a hundred years ago and requires the same number of musicians. In short, productivity does not advance in orchestras very much to offset the continuous rise in labor costs. A one percent cost advance in the wage bill per year would compound to thirtyfive percent total increase over a thirty year period whereas the real cost of many competing goods would advance by much less because of productivity improvements. Orchestras, and performing arts organizations generally, face the full pressures of rising labor costs not typical to the bulk of the economy. If admission fees rose at the same rate as labor costs, the public would tend to shift their spending to relatively less pricey goods. A saving grace fortunately helps to sustain symphony attendance. If symphony performances

---

[13] W. J. Baumol and W. G. Bowen, "On the Performing Arts: The Anatomy of Their Economic Problems," *American Economic Review* 55, no. 1/2 (1965).

constitute a luxury good that people desire more of as their real spending power advances, then ticket prices can indeed be increased and patrons with growing wealth can afford to also increase voluntary contributions. Whether a balance will be sustained between the two forces, rising costs on one hand and rising patron incomes on the other, remains a challenge performing arts organizations will always face, and they, like museums, will always have to worry about covering their fixed costs for which admission fees can do only part of the job.

***

Both symphony orchestras and museums face existential challenges not just from costs, but from harmful current attendance trends as well. Millennials in particular attend at lesser rates than older patrons such "signature arts events" as jazz and classical music concerts, musicals, plays, and art museum and gallery exhibits. Of such events, operas and symphony orchestras have suffered the most in attendance problems. Between 2007 and 2009, annual opera attendance dropped from 7.5 million to 4.3 million, and symphony orchestra attendance remained flat at about 25 million after peaking in 2006 at about 28 million. Age plays an especially important role in explaining attendance at museums[14] and classical music concerts,[15] activities that depend more on older attendees than do jazz concerts and musical theater. Millennials do spend less than their elders on entertainment as one would expect given their more modest incomes and accumulated wealth, and, indeed, statistical analysis shows that a lower income negatively affects individual attendance rates at signature cultural events along with a younger age.[16] In 2009 average consumer spending on entertainment and reading equaled about $2,700. Those under 25 spent an average of $1,200 while 25-34 year olds spent $2,600.[17] Simply put, whether they would like to attend or not, Millennials

---

[14] Ibid.
[15] National Endowment for The Arts, "How a Nation Engages with Art: Highlights from the 2012 Survey of Public Participation in the Arts."
[16] Victoria M. Ateca-Amestoy and Juan Prieto-Rodriguez, "Forecasting Accuracy of Behavioural Models for Participation in the Arts," in *ACEI Working Paper Series* (Oviedo, Spain: Association for Cultural Economics, 2011).
[17] National Endowment for The Arts, "How a Nation Engages with Art: Highlights from the 2012 Survey of Public Participation in the Arts," (Washington D.C.: National Endowment for the Arts, 2014).

lack the financial capacity currently to save the day for those high-admission-cost traditional arts institutions suffering admissions shrinkage due to aging audiences.

One might infer that their low attendance rates at "signature arts events" means that Millennials lack a strong attachment to the arts, but this would be a big mistake. Millennials in fact undertake such creative activities as classical music performance, painting, photography, and creative writing at greater rates than their elders. In short, Millennials actively participate in the arts more extensively than others, and will be more often found performing on stage or displaying their art at local galleries than their older peers. Despite their scarcity at "signature" classical music concerts, the rate of attendance at "any live musical performance" is much greater for Millennials than other adults. Millennials love music, just not necessarily the kind favored by their parents and grandparents. In 2012 the rate of attendance at a live musical performance was 41 percent for ages 18-24, 34 percent for 25-34, and 32 percent for adults as a whole. The three most popular venues in order for such performances were parks or open-air settings, theaters or concert halls or auditoriums, and restaurants, bars, nightclubs, or coffee shops. Given their special affinity for digital technology, Millennials download music, books, and other cultural objects to a much greater extent than everyone else. In sum, Millennials access substantial amounts of culture digitally, engage in hands-on arts activities more extensively than older others, but attend key traditional cultural events, such as costly art museum exhibits and symphony concerts, at lower rates than the rest of the adult population. To repeat, Millennials attend musical concerts of all types more often than other adults, but they take special advantage of free or low cost performances in central city parks, bars, coffee shops, and other venues. Despite their lower incomes, they are surprisingly more frequent participants in art object purchases than others, although no doubt at the less expensive end of the market.[18]

In virtue of their special desire for opportunities to both engage in and enjoy the visual and performing arts, Millennials unsurprisingly choose more than most to live in central cities.

---

[18]Ibid.

Simply put, urban centers are where the action is. Artists of all types congregate in neighborhoods where they can best find affordable housing, workspaces, and venues for their creations and performances, and these occur predominantly in central cities.[19] While the traditional arts institutions attract older empty nesters, younger adults seek out the more offbeat and less costly visual and performing arts available in local venues. Millennials access much of their social and cultural life with the touch of a finger online, but like all of us they periodically desire a live, shared, and physically direct experience of cultural activities, and they want them close at hand. The seeking of such cultural experiences by post-materialist Millennials is indeed a boon to the resurgence of older urban centers.

***

Shared experience in compact central cities extends beyond conscious participation in cultural activities to the more ordinary task of both purposeful getting around as well as aimless but pleasurable wandering about. Both of course can be carried out in either spread-out suburbs or compact urban centers, but how exactly does the experience of moving around by car in the suburbs compare with using public transit, walking, or biking in the central city? A car is convenient and physically comfortable. You don't have to worry about being exposed to the elements in a car, and you can often easily and quickly drive right up to your final destination. But a car entraps you if you get stuck in traffic and isolates you from others around you. Such isolation can encourage destructive and antisocial behavior such as dangerous and uncaring driving and road rage. Biking gives you a lot of flexibility to go around traffic, exercises your body, and offers a unique visual and sensual experience induced by direct interaction with your spatial and physical environment. Such interaction has its own dangers, especially if you like biking fast or taking risks dodging traffic. Walking is a similar experience, but occurs at a much slower pace and puts you in more direct contact with others allowing for a certain amount of vicarious sociality and the occasional unplanned encounter with known others. Both biking and walking are especially problematic in bad weather, and

---

[19]See Chapter 5.

walking particularly can take too long for lengthy trips. Buses or light rail cars also offers opportunities for inadvertent social encounters, but more than one might want when crowding occurs or rambunctious school kids get on. The nice thing about mass transit is that one can read a book or play with one's cell phone while moving about without endangering others, or you can gaze out the window and daydream if you want. The big frustration with mass transit apart from crowding is excessive wait times and a system that doesn't always take you where you want to go. There is of course the "bus people," those who suffer lives on society's margins and sometimes exhibit undesirable behaviors, but who are also sometimes interesting to observe or even talk to.

I am not sure how this all balances out in the end. If you want comfort, convenience, safety, or power, or to exhibit status, you better drive and pay the price of traffic congestion and social isolation. If you have a sense of adventure, give the other ways of getting around a whirl. The virtue of high-density living is you can mix them all up and add variety to your life experiences. In the last 100 hundred years, suburbs and motor vehicles won the competitive struggle for consumer loyalties. More recently, the choice of where to live and how to get around is moving back modestly toward compact central cities and against motor vehicles, and post-materialist Millennials are leading the way. This amounts to a virtuous shift towards less entropic and less economically materialistic forms of life's experiences.

10 Post-Material Philosophy

Anyone who has taken modern philosophy courses may come away scratching their head about how philosophical thought matters at all for how we live. We now see that a post-material philosophical orientation makes a difference for our economic, social, and political life, but we haven't said much about what academic philosophy can tell us about the virtues and content of post-materialism. While many modern philosophers wouldn't pay much attention to this question, from those that do we can come up with a collection of interesting ideas that give more intellectual heft to post-materialism. I find this to be a useful and interesting exercise, but you may not. You can just move on to the final chapters, but I would hope instead that you rise to the challenge of philosophical thinking.

***

Friedrich Nietzsche, a cranky but brainy German philosopher who lived and wrote in the last half of the Nineteenth Century, wanted nothing to do with worries about final causes or pre-cooked religious explanations about ethics or the meaning of life. In his eyes freedom and autonomy are the central values to live by and meaning is to be sought in the experience of earthly existence. Religion is a con, a way for a priestly class to gain power over others, and ought to be chucked in favor of artistic expression as the medium for reconciling the sufferings and wonders of life. Simply put, in his thinking Nietzsche gives content to the bones of what today we call post-materialism, as we will now see.

The Greeks expressed two great themes in life: the beauty, power, and creativity of the human individual and the inevitability of deep and personal tragedy in the course of historical and personal events. The first took form in the plastic arts, in statues and temples, and the second in the Greek theater, in the performance of plays written in competitions to win the hearts of Greek audiences. The Greek spring theater festival commemorated Dionysus, the god of wine, a contradictory figure who at once purveyed the joys and ecstasies of life but also took pleasure in the chase of living beings and their dismemberment by his lovely maenads who otherwise danced and flitted through the woods in ecstatic reverie. If nothing else, the Greeks are realists in the creation of their gods. Wine brings forth pleasure but also the dark ravings and destructiveness of dangerous drunks. Wine and celebration dulls life's rough edges but also can destroy its tranquility and beauty. Tragedy thus was a fitting theme for celebrating the emergence of new branches on the grapevine and the mixed blessing of the coming new wines.

The contrast of Apollonian orderly beauty and Dionysian ecstatic reverie in Greek art and thought Friedrich Nietzsche describes brilliantly in his first book, *The Birth of Tragedy*.[1] On the topic of tragic pain and suffering, he knew of what he spoke. Illnesses, including migraines, deteriorating vision, and digestion problems, caused him to retire early from his professorship and kept him from studying and writing more than a few hours a day. He also sadly suffered from depression and mental disorders that eventually drove him insane.

Western thinking is wrongly dominated in Nietzsche's eyes by Socratic rational elements that exclude our darker non-rational side that takes form in a fear of death, a deep passion for life's pleasures, and the submergence of individuality within a larger being. The striving for continued existence, the exercise of the animal instincts, the lust for sexual union, and the mystery of death all possess an amazing power over our emotional lives. Just like the Greek god Dionysus, we want to immerse ourselves in elemental life forces, forget our individuality, and become one with the ecstasies of earthly being, but the danger is that such passions can get out of control and seek satisfaction in the barbarisms of rape, pillage, and murder that we see all too often in the daily news.

The opposing and equally powerful tendency, to rationalize existence and explain it in logical terms, is manifested in Apollo, the Greek god of light, dreams, and plastic energy whose essence is captured by artists in sculpted, idealistic images that exhibit order, tranquility, and control. Apollo symbolizes a regulated beauty and contentment seen by Nietzsche as an illusion given the

---

[1]Friedrich Nietzsche, "The Birth of Tragedy: Out of the Spirit of Music," in *Basic Writings of Nietzsche*, ed. Walter Kaufmann (New York: Random House, 2000).

reality of tragic suffering and death, but an illusion that we all deeply desire. Otherwise, life's intrinsic pain would be too hard to bear. We dream of a predictable and beautiful world, and Apollo symbolizes that dream. Life for the Greek philosopher Socrates is Apollonian in its quest for truth through logical thought and orderly being. Wrong actions are the result of imperfect knowledge and good actions emerge from clear thinking; knowledge is virtue and the virtuous are happy.

In the original staging of Greek tragedy, the citizens of Athens shared a ceremonial and dramatic reconciliation with life's realities. Rather than narcissistically focusing on their individual plights, Athenians found collective dignity and joy in stories about life's deep sadness. We humans long for connection with the primitive, the natural, and the wild, for an ecstatic union with a worldly whole where we can forget our troubles. We would like to believe that we can control and shape the world and that doing so serves the end of our happiness. In reality we are limited beings with a modest capacity to determine our own destiny. Hard as it may be, we need to accept the cruelties of human existence and our individual limitations and find solace in earthly wonders. This is where joy and contentment come in—connection to the world and acceptance of our historical fate. Despite the horrors of daily life, we have little choice but to plunge ahead and do something that occupies our creative impulses. The collective experience of theatrical tragedy driven by the haunting music of the chorus helped the Greeks do just that. Music especially emotionally binds us to the group and lets us forget about our individual vulnerabilities. Psychologically it can put us in a trance and send us off to the heavens. For me personally, chamber music does the trick, but in our own times, the best example for most might be a rock concert, judging from audience behavior at such events. Any public gathering based on a shared experience give us an uplifting sense of connection to the human totality—baseball games, political rallies, plays (including Greek tragedies), and musical performances. We come away cleansed of daily irritations and feeling that life is good and worth living (unless maybe our team loses). Sporting events and political rallies satisfy our instincts to warrior competitiveness, and the performance arts our quest for beauty and order as well inoculation from life's pains and horrors. Public rituals and their underlying shared values create feelings of affinity and commitment within a society. After such events, one can return to daily life with a renewed energy to take on not only the ordinary, but also those Apollonian projects that give life an orderly grace and rationality. We indeed need a little 'Greek cheerfulness,' something that can give us comfort and joy in our personal lives to accompany our collective bond to the larger community and our reconciliation with our suffering and mortality. These are messages of *The Birth of Tragedy*.

Nietzsche's early thinking pivots on an interplay between individualistic creative impulses and the desire for a collective connection, but this is not to last. With the disappearance of Dionysian elements central to *The Birth of Tragedy* in his later writings, he turns to an individualistic, anti-metaphysical, and empirically oriented philosophy in such works as *Human, All-To-Human, The Dawn of Day,* and *The Gay Science*.[2] Understanding comes for him not from some other-worldly, overarching notion of a final cause, but through a close attention to the reality around us and a careful and critical assessment of humanity's social constructs and beliefs. Life in the world flows from interrelated chains of deterministic causalities, not from some singular underlying fundamental force. Quasi-religious, oceanic, or mystical feelings rooted in public spectacles or religious or artistic experiences are fine, but they tell us nothing about reality, other than the presence of a human inclination to such feelings. The need for collective connection to salve fears of suffering and death lacks earthly importance for the later Nietzsche in comparison to the significance of individual self-creation, to which the energies of our wilder Dionysian urges for sensual experiences and holistic merging are now to be sublimated, redirected, and put to good use.

This task constitutes a self-overcoming, a steering of one's emotional urges towards artistic and intellectual productivity. Out of this exercise in self-control arise the values that we should live

---

[2]Friedrich Nietzsche, *Human, All-Too-Human*, trans. Helen Zimmern and Paul V. Cohn (Lawrence: Digireads.com, 2009); Friedrich Nietzsche, *The Dawn of Day*, trans. J. M. Kennedy (London: Dover, 2007); Friedrich Nietzsche, *The Gay Science*, ed. Bernard Williams, trans. Josefine Nauckhoff and Adrian Del Caro (Cambridge: Cambridge University Press, 2001).

by—courage, self-discipline, hardness, and intellectual integrity. One's personal life is like a work of art and should be consciously molded and shaped accordingly. We have to accept the fundamentals of who we are—our inner drives, our skills and talents, and our limitations—but we then must have the courage and will to consciously shape what we do in life. We shouldn't simply accept whatever society lays out for us as an income earner or consumer. If you don't like crunching numbers, avoid becoming an accountant. If you find the suburbs boring, take a chance and move to a more exciting but gritty central city. All this requires individual self-assertion and discipline, the opposite of succumbing to safe comforts and group conformity. Don't spend your life resenting and seeking revenge for what history has laid on you; focus instead on that one striving most stimulating to your passion and concern, and organize your being around it. This is the essence of Nietzsche's advice, not too different what one would find in the popular psychology section of a bookstore today. Self-creation in Nietzsche's eyes is only for those with a capacity to become "free spirits," a select group of elite thinkers willing to go against the social grain in their advocacy for new and unpopular ideas. "Free spirits" lead the charge in formulating unpopular but necessary alternatives to ossified and failed social traditions and institutions.

Nietzsche himself fills the bill as a "free spirit" in his unrelenting and lifelong attack on Christianity. The "death of God" claim, for which he is famous, refers uniquely to a Christian God and a doctrine that devalues actual existence in favor of a hypothetical and unproven afterlife. Faith in God and charity towards others in this life will be eternally rewarded in the next. One gives to a homeless beggar or the Salvation Army bell ringer at Christmas not out of fellow feeling, but from a fear of Godly retribution for being uncharitable, a sense of shame for being ungenerous, or the psychic satisfaction from feelings of economic superiority over recipients. The homeless beggar in turn experiences the indignity of having to rely on the charity of others. Nietzsche infers that charity of any kind, Christian or otherwise, blunts the desire for self-reliance, independence, and accomplishment, and insidiously debilitates cultural motivations for progress and achievement. Focusing on the next life supports the institutions of Christianity at the ultimate cost of weakening the cultural fabric of this life.

Although Nietzsche vigorously attacked modern Christianity, he recognized the need for tradition as social glue essential for group survival in a world of conflict and competition. The medieval church, with the mystery of its ritual and the power of its priesthood to offer forgiveness of sins and entry into heaven, kept the peasantry under control and working hard to supply economic sustenance to religious elites and their aristocratic allies. Christian charity not only kept the church afloat, but also provided a safety net to the peasantry in hard times. For the majority of a society's population, what Nietzsche dismissively calls "the herd," obedience to the Christian tradition was essential for basic order in Medieval times, but in a changing world, such traditions lose their punch and new values are required to prevent cultural decline. In a modern capitalist society, economic discipline depends less on religious and more on economic reward. Belief in God and an afterlife loses its motivational functionality in today's consumer economy where more immediate benefits drive economic behavior.

In his explanation of how societies change and evolve, Nietzsche is a Darwinian. For survival, communities rely on a binding faith embodied in customs and traditions that create the order and civility essential for social survival. As a matter of habit individuals obey unwritten rules that limit harm to others in daily interaction and commit everyone to the defense of the community against outside oppression. We must not only be willing to hold doors for others and refrain from stealing wallets sticking out of back pockets, but to take up arms against our enemies if needed. From time to time, the basic tenants of the underlying binding faith lose their effectiveness, requiring the death of old traditions and the birth of new, and it is the "free spirits," those iconoclasts contemptuous of existing social arrangements, who successfully seek out new schemes essential for continued social progress. The values postulated in his day, especially by the church, were repulsive to Nietzsche, who saw in them as no more than a means for social domination. The "death of God" meant concretely to him the rejection of an existing religious dogma that, in its commitment to faith and charity, sapped the worldly passion for progress and creativity.

The notion of self-creating free spirits, who bring forth radically new schemes of social organization, doesn't jibe very well with Nietzsche's commitment to deterministic and naturalistic causal chains as key to understanding how the world works. If human life is a product of a Darwinian natural and historical determinism, then how can free spirits ever act to radically alter human values and change the course of history? One answer is the insertion of the "free spirit" as an adaptive force for change much like a genetic mutation. In a Darwinian social world, the probability of any "free spirit" causing dramatic historical shifts may well be infinitesimal but nonetheless positive just as the probability of any genetic mutation being evolutionarily adaptive is positive but very small. Cultural memes, ideas, symbols, and social practices that survive and get transmitted within a society from one person to another, bubble up in a random fashion much like adaptive genetic mutations. What a given free spirit accomplishes in creating such memes really doesn't matter much, but some one among many free-spirited ideas may stick and become the start of a larger social trend. With a sufficient number of functioning free spirits, chances are that someone will come up a new culturally adaptive value scheme essential to stave off social decline. A Darwinian world, whether biological or cultural, is still deterministic, but free spirits become a part of the adaptive dynamic through creation of cultural mutations. Whether Nietzsche was thinking in these terms I can't say. He may have inferred as much in the subtitle to his crowning literary achievement, *Thus Spoke Zarathustra: A Book for All and None*.[3] All of us should become the overman and creators of new notions, although no one of us is likely to be the one that changes the world, but we each have a shot at it. Modern reconciliations of free will and causal determinism places human rationality and intentionality within nature's causal determinism, and this Nietzsche accomplishes in his Darwinian take on evolutionary social change.

---

[3]Friedrich Nietzsche, *Thus Spoke Zarathustra: A Book for None and All*, trans. Walter Kaufmann (New York: Penguin Books, 1978).

Aside from a commitment to free spirited self-creation and the death of heavenly explanations for being, Nietzsche is famous for a second theme, "the will to power," an idea that has received two interpretations, one benign and one insidious. At one level will to power is a self-overcoming, the guiding and directing of basic passions to productive ends. Self-creation of this kind requires a degree of will to power, but Nietzsche goes further and proclaims that there is within our earthly existence "will to power, and nothing besides." In this formulation, all of life becomes an exercise in self-expansion, power, and domination for individuals and societies alike. In his most foreboding work, *Beyond Good and Evil*, this idea takes on a special prominence.[4] In watching daily television newscasts on worldly events, one can easily become convinced that Nietzsche might be right.

For Nietzsche, a focus on will to power in some of his writings is more an experiment than an overarching commitment to a singular vision of human motivation. Throughout his intellectual career he tried ideas on for size and discarded those that didn't wear well. Some he simply put in the closet for later use, but as one Nietzsche scholar convincingly argues, "will to power" is not among them. The rise and fall of Nietzsche's commitment to will to power is chronicled in a chapter of a must-read book for anyone interested in philosophy, Julian Young's *Friedrich Nietzsche: A Philosophical Biography*.[5] Most tellingly, Nietzsche wrote over a thousand pages of notes on will to power but never published his planned crowning achievement on the topic. Nietzsche's sister Elizabeth deviously published a badly edited version, *The Will to Power: Attempt at Revaluation of All Values*, for her own ideological purposes after his death.[6] Otherwise, will to power as a singular notion explaining natural and historical evolution takes up very few of Nietzsche's published pages. That there is "will to power and nothing else" seems to be one of the ideas he tried on for size but ultimately rejected. Philosophers who achieve intellectual fame, such as Plato and Kant, are "systematizers" who

---

[4]Nietzsche, "Beyond Good and Evil: Prelude to a Philosophy of the Future."
[5]Julian Young, *Friedrich Nietzsche: A Philosophical Biography* (Cambridge: Cambridge University Press, 2010).
[6]Friedrich Nietzsche, *Will to Power*, trans. Anthony M. Ludovici (New York2006).

create frameworks that claim to explain existence in comprehensive terms. Although he clamored for the recognition accorded systematizers, Nietzsche's deep intellectual integrity caused him to reject such an approach: "I mistrust all systematizers and go out of my way to avoid them."[7] The complexity and richness of the observed world precludes simplistic explanations and moves him to give up on will to power as an overarching idea of how things hang together. In *Twilight of the Idols*, one of his final published works, he expresses a renewed commitment to the behavioral dualism of the Dionysian urge for connection and the Apollonian impulse for individual creativity he originally described in *The Birth of Tragedy*.[8] Will to power remains in his thinking as a force behind personal self-overcoming and the impulse to free artistic and intellectual expression, but never fully takes hold as a final explanation of all organic and inorganic phenomena in the observed world. The path of human flourishing for Nietzsche is ultimately to be defined by a community's own invented virtues from which the brutal exercise of unbridled power will be excluded. Saying yes to life, no matter how tragic it may be, connects us to a world beyond the self. We follow our individual inclinations and desires, but among those is a need to further the continuation of life in whatever way we can, a force embodied in the overflowing power of the collective Dionysian urges. This is the final message of *Twilight of the Idols*, the single most compact statement of Nietzsche's philosophy.

The biggest flaw in Nietzsche's thinking for modern day liberals would be his attitude toward the masses of humanity, or as he called them, "the herd." The inference of the term is that the vast majority of human beings engage in a herd-like allegiance to cultural beliefs, in his day to a mindless Christianity, today perhaps to a mindless consumerism. He also refers to societies as a motley but uninteresting collection of cultural practices that lead nowhere. Nietzsche's essential goal was to be the one to lead western society to a promised land of recreated, coherent human values much as

---

[7]Young, *Friedrich Nietzsche: A Philosophical Biography*. See page 542. He expresses a similar sentiment in *Twilight of the Idols:* "I mistrust all systematizers and avoid them. The will to a system is a lack of integrity."
[8]Ibid. See pages 497-503; Friedrich Nietzsche, *Twilight of the Idols* (Oxford: Oxford University Press, 1998).

his fictional guru in *Thus Spoke Zarathustra*.[9] It is only the overman, the talented "free spirit," that is capable of pulling off leading the herd to becoming one with the earth and giving up on heavenly rewards. For Nietzsche, it is Earth itself that contains all the wonders of being, and it is a human responsibility to preserve, enjoy, and advance earthly beauties and delights. This is the essence of Zarathustra's message. It is Earth that is sacred, not the heavens. The real ambiguity in Nietzsche's thinking is the role of society's masses, or what he refers to as the "herd." Are they simply servants of free spirits? Cogs in an industrial wheel of material production? Nietzsche neither much liked the mechanisms of industrial capitalism nor trusted the state to bring about human liberation. He unrealistically suggests at one point that Europe's industrial masses seek their freedom through emigration to America without really understanding that industrialism there differed little from Europe's. With his belief in democracy as a force for rule by the averageness of the herd, Nietzsche doesn't leave advocates of democratic pluralism much to go on. In the end, he calls not for democracy, but a society that serves a free-spirited philosophical elite, a vision not conceptually different from Plato's state ruled by a philosopher king. One could equally argue that a democratized world of free spirits, where everyone is self-creative and possesses the potential to produce adaptive social mutations, would lead more smoothly and consistently to positive social change than would a monopoly of elites. To come up with the notion of tolerance and equal rights for gays or protecting nature's wonders doesn't require a genius, just people who are clever and persistent, traits that I imagine are fairly widespread within humanity.

How do you know when life has achieved its self-creative purpose? Nietzsche offers us a mental exercise to establish just this. Suppose you are told that you will experience your life in its every detail repeatedly in a never-ending cycle. Would you view this news with absolute horror or overpowering joy? This is an expression of Nietzsche's doctrine of the "eternal return of the same." If this question evokes positive feeling, then you must be close to your self-creative goal. Most of us do things we seriously

---

[9] Nietzsche, *Thus Spoke Zarathustra: A Book for None and All*.

regret, but if we can look back on our life as a whole and judge it positively, we have done the best we can. Nietzsche's eternal return is a tough taskmaster most of us can never perfectly satisfy. Nonetheless, Zarathustra in Nietzsche's crowning literary work experiences spiritual and Dionysian visions of eternal return through an ecstatic connection to his free-spirited disciples, as imperfect in practice as they were. Nietzsche here closes his own intellectual circle with a return to the idea of submergence in the whole. In an act of self-overcoming we are to organize our life around a singular mission that links us to the historical fate of the world around us. Our chosen mission, would allow us to will eternal return, not just for ourselves, but also for all that exists. My reading of this point goes something like this: choose a mission for your life that you believe would be good beyond your own self; organize you life around that mission; while having an ultimate faith that your hopes will be realized, bear no illusions that your personal accomplishments will make much difference, but retain a lifelong commitment to the end you seek. No matter how painful and fearful life is, to it one must always say yes. In Nietzsche's eyes, this is the essential message of the Greeks who individually and collectively celebrated human perseverance, heroism, and perfection in the face of overwhelming cruelty and tragedy.

Nietzsche's aphoristic style of writing, although engaging, challenges the reader to come up with a coherent vision of what he is up to. About this, there is much debate, but I personally find Martin Heidegger's conclusion on Nietzsche in *What is Called Thinking?* to be especially useful.[10] According to Heidegger, the central message of *Thus Spoke Zarathustra* is that man is unready to assume responsibility for the power of industry and technology and as a result is turning the earth into a "wasteland." Man is not yet capable of thinking clearly about his existential reality and is still prone to look beyond the earth to the heavens for his salvation. Nietzsche's clear-thinking "overman" will instead look to the realities of life on earth in the creation of meaning, not to the unreality of an afterlife in the great beyond. True "free spirits" will seek not just their personal pleasures, but will set the earth itself up

---

[10]Martin Heidegger, *What is Called Thinking?* , trans. J. Glenn Gray (New York: Harper, 1976).

as a truly sacred being to be respected and loved. Its not too much of a stretch to claim that Zarathustra was an environmental philosopher who, by proclaiming the death of God, wants to pull our attention back to the wonders of the world in which we actually live. The "overman" will be both a humanist and environmentalist and therefore a post-material universalist.

If Nietzsche lived today, where would he find his "free spirits?" Given his passion for the arts, especially for music, he would doubtlessly check out the post-materialists bringing new energy and artistic accomplishment to some of our older central cities. Here he might find fascination with the emergent quest for creative accomplishment in both the arts and digital arenas, growing distaste for conformity to the materialist values, Dionysian desire for unique collective and personal experiences, and growing advocacy for free personal expression. He might be pleasantly surprised by post-materialism's combination of stylistic nonconformity and traditional commitment to hard work and merit-based reward at places like Google and Facebook. While Nietzsche would not find the democratic informality of the digital world very appealing, he might like its creativity and unconventionality. While Google seems to at least give lip service to respecting and protecting the earth's wonders, whether the Google folks satisfy Nietzsche's vision of the overman as a protector of the Earth we cannot say.

While he always fascinates in his writings, Nietzsche doesn't always leave much for the soul. As close as he comes is his talk of "spiritualizing" our basic human drives for sex and love, warfare, or ecstatic communal celebrations instead of sublimating and suppressing such urges in deference to some distant, heavenly god and unnatural morality. Much like the Greeks, who created their gods in their own image, sexual promiscuities and all, Nietzsche calls for a humanized spirituality. He speaks of the Earth itself in sacred tones and wants it treated as such, and he emphatically says yes to earthly life as tragic and painful as it can be. To traditional religionists, such talk would be a sacrilege, but not so much to post-materialists who express a spirituality unattached to any particular doctrine. Martin Heidegger, another controversial but brilliant German philosopher, who also mistrusts metaphysicians and systematizers, takes Nietzsche's notion of a philosophy and spirituality rooted in the realities of daily life even further, as we will now see. Stay tuned.

***

Being a post-materialist means that in deciding how to live one goes beyond a narrow focus on private economic interests to include such purposes as individual self-expression, social tolerance, and a quality environment. While suspicious of organize religion, many post-materialists adhere to an unstructured form of spirituality and express a sense of the sacred. For this reason, it is time to extend our philosophy for the future to account for such an emotional attachment to something larger than the self. The one philosopher that accomplishes this while avoiding the metaphysics of final causality or reliance on belief in a creator is Martin Heidegger. We will see in Heidegger's writings a philosophy that treats the everyday universe of perception with a non-religious spiritual reverence and a deep conviction that calls out for the preservation of both humanity's and nature's earthly wonders.

Most of us rarely think about what 'being in the world' truly means and leave such questions to academics or theologians. We need to get on with our daily lives where most of the issues we face are pragmatic. For philosophically oriented speculative thinkers, to ask about the nature of being is the most elevated of all questions, but also the most difficult to grasp. To emphasize the importance of the question, let's follow Heidegger and capitalize 'Being' just as it is our common practice to capitalize 'God' when we speak of beliefs in a final creator. Particular beings include all the phenomenon of human experience—Cormorants diving for fish in Lake Michigan, light reflecting on water from a morning sun peaking through the clouds, bikers head to work on a bike trail, the taste of espresso, and whatever else enters your consciousness. We can postulate one common element of all such beings without getting into too much philosophical trouble—all things in our field of perception exist at the moment we observe them. Being in this sense refers to the active presence of an endless array of particular objects and their interconnections, but not to any abstract, and probably unanswerable, questions about ultimate cause. In making this claim, we direct our attention to the perceived as such and to the simple amazement of its existence. This I think is what

Heidegger is up to, but I will leave the final judgment about this to you once we summarize some of his philosophical ideas.

For Martin Heidegger, to ask about the nature of Being is to look closely at life as we find it. He grew up in intensely Catholic and conservative early Twentieth Century rural southern Germany where his father was a master cooper and sexton of the local Catholic Church. Heidegger's education through the university level was paid for by the Church, with the expectation that he was destined for the clergy. At the university in Freiburg, he shifted from preparation for the priesthood to the study of Catholic philosophy, receiving a scholarship from the church in support of his work. Heidegger rejected Catholicism soon after World War I and moved on to become a student of the phenomenologist Edmund Husserl, gaining a position as a professor at (the Protestant) Marburg University and ultimately succeeding Husserl at Freiburg in 1928. By this time Heidegger's lectures in philosophy were the stuff of legend in German intellectual circles.

Heidegger published his much anticipated book, *Being and Time*, in 1927.[11] Here he sets out the work that is to occupy him for the rest of his life, the sorting out of the meaning of being in the world. To a pragmatic thinker, this would seem to be a self-indulgent exercise in abstract theorizing, but what Heidegger attempts to create is a philosophy of everyday life, a task that begins with sorting out the significance of the different objects we encounter. Those that rise to particular importance are the "ready-to-hand," the tools of existence—hammers, plows, houses, computers, cups and saucers, coats and pants, guitars, baseballs, and so on. The rest of the things we encounter, the "present-at-hand," lay in the background of our lives and fail to attract our attention because we don't care much about them—beetles, sphagnum moss on forest trees, boulders, discarded plastic bags. Something of little interest to us at one point in our life may take on a special significance at another; a rock of a certain size becomes especially important to me when I want to pound tent stakes into the ground on camping trips. We approach any object in our attention span with "circumspection." How can we use

---

[11]Martin Heidegger, *Being and Time*, trans. John Macquarrie and Edward Robinson (Oxford: Blackwell, 1962).

it? Will it harm us in some way? Is it pleasing? How does it function? What does it do? How do I avoid it or get around it?

Given the social nature of human experience, our encounters with human-others, as opposed to objects, takes on a special importance, and is referred to as "being-with." One's everyday life consists of a complex of interrelationships with others—spouses, children, grocers, car mechanics, beauticians, baristas, friends, lovers, fellow workers, softball teammates. We approach these individuals with "solicitude." How do others react to my behavior? Do I trust someone? Am I sexually attracted to a particular person? Is my softball teammate a skilled player? Does this barista make really good espresso? How can I help my son become less depressed? Is the police officer following me going to give me a ticket? Will I be assaulted if a go into a particular neighborhood? Will my friends be at the coffee shop today?

The vast majority of our relations in the world, both with humans and nonhuman objects, take on an ordinary quality, or "everydayness." I get up, have breakfast with my wife, maybe talk about plans for the day, read some of the newspaper, go exercise, head to the coffee shop, haul out my computer to do some writing (I am retired), go home for lunch, chat and gossip with people I know at another coffee shop, read some philosophy, shop at the grocery store, fix dinner, talk to my wife about my day, and so on. These are the repetitive, ordinary tasks of daily existence. In them, one life looks much like another; nothing distinguishes us or causes us to stand out. We gain enjoyment from many of these activities and connections, although not all. I love conversing with friends on the horrible state of politics or the economy, or talking to the barista about the finer points of making espresso, but I am not so keen about calming my son's anxieties around having to learn college level economic theory, or having to speak with a neighbor about a dent I put in his car when backing out of my driveway. I enjoy fixing dinner and having a glass of wine while doing so, and I like catching the evening news. Some of what we do may be quite boring, although necessary to daily life—washing the dishes, getting the laundry done, painting the deck, commuting on a congested expressway, serving the fiftieth cup of coffee to our customers at work, and numerous other tasks you can imagine for yourself. Of course boredom and its lack is partly a matter of taste—I thoroughly enjoy hanging laundry outdoors on a summer's day, something many think to be intrinsically mundane.

Your hackles may rise at the idea that the ordinary experiences that take up much of our earthly existence are "inauthentic," but that's what Heidegger calls them. He does this not to denigrate the ordinary. After all, most of the events of our life are pretty ordinary, but that doesn't mean they are unnecessary or that they don't bring us joy. I love my daily espresso, but that doesn't mean it's anything special in the bigger scheme of things. Ordinary life can be good, but it isn't what gives us our unique identity. What does this is "the authentic," that generally rare kind of activity that causes us to stand out from the crowd and puts into practice our own, self-determined philosophy of life. To live fully, is to both live in everyday inauthenticity and to express one's idiosyncratic and "authentic" self.

The essential human motivation underlying both the everyday and the authentic is "care." As already noted, we approach life with circumspection, concern, and solicitousness. We care about those things and those persons in the environment around us that we take to be important. We fear having the things we need and the people close to us torn away. There is nothing necessarily altruistic in the idea of care. Care can be about the self; one can care deeply about avoiding muggers lying in wait in dark alleys, or a homeless person can feel serious concern about where her next meal will come from; or care can be for the well-being of others close to us, or for the place or community in which we live, or for things in the natural world we have come to love like wildflowers and beautiful landscapes. Care is an existential feature of life. I care; therefore I am.

Closely related to care is the idea of "anxiety." Anxiousness is a kind of nebulous fear about "not-being," about being a nothing rather than a something. One goes through daily life without thinking much about nonexistence, but in reflective moments one suddenly becomes fearful of not living, or, more to the point, not having lived in a significant way. We become worried about sinking into the obscurity of the average in our daily being. This is the source of our inherent, if often hidden, desire to go beyond everydayness and seek something authentic. Anxiety generates a particular form of care—a special concern about having a personal existence that is uniquely valuable. Recognizing the possibility of "not-being" creates anxiety about finitude in our lives, but its flip side, the mere fact that beings exist, can also create "astonishment" and wonder. Such astonishment is as fundamental as anxiety. We awake each day with a feeling of anxiousness about what it is we should do, or with a feeling of amazement that we exist in a world where the sun shines through our window, or maybe both. Out of our conflicting emotions, we carve out a balance between care for everydayness and a passion for something special, that is, if we are both resolute and lucky.

Authenticity in its essence is subjective. We can debate about what an authentic life is like, but we cannot establish final standards to describe it. One can speak of authenticity in a general way, but not be able to say for sure if this or that person attains it. Whether one's own actions are authentic is a matter of reflective, honest self-judgment. We can, and do in our public discourse, look at the lives of others and argue about the character of their actions. Read newspapers, websites, and advertisements—most say something about questions of personal authenticity. People whose lives have authentic elements get written about, but not so much those stuck in inauthenticity. Who would admit to living a mundane life of total everydayness? People do own up to unhappiness in the extensive survey research on the subject, but do unhappiness and inauthenticity go together? One can be dumb and happy, as the saying goes, one could be inauthentic and happy as well, or even authentic and miserable. The best way to describe the authentic is that unique part of our own life that we pursue as a matter of passion and special commitment. The authentic rises above the mundane and becomes a special kind of activity, an act of free expression. This doesn't mean that we escape everydayness in our existence; it simply means that at some moments we engage in something more. We are all moved to live authentically, but some no doubt do this more successfully than others. This is why we take such an interest in the topic. We all in some way want to stand out and express our own individuality, but we also enjoy submerging ourselves into the comforting routine of our everyday being.

Both everydayness and authenticity exist in the context of concrete daily existence and thus possess "historicality." To speak about history from the individual's perspective is to talk about a unified self that exists over time. At the core of our identity is a selfsameness we create by knitting together sequences of experiences into a kind of personal narrative. We desperately want to have a story we can tell others that expresses the meaning of our particular existence. This is how we become historical.

For the most part, we exist within the facts of history. Our possibilities are given to us by what our culture and time delivers up. We are tossed into a world not of our making, but in this world we can behave resolutely and rise above everydayness by committing ourselves to a heritage, a certain set of time-tested practices. We are compelled by fate to take the plate we are given, but we can choose what we take from it. In short, we can't alter history writ large, but we can shape our own personal destiny within it.

In accepting a tradition we buy into a certain vision of how a particular kind of life should be lived. Some traditions deserve to die, even to be destroyed. Choosing from history's plate can be exceedingly dangerous without an intense and open public debate about what should be rejected out of hand. Any tradition with the clear potential to demean, enslave, and destroy human and other natural beings on its face is a candidate for such rejection. Heidegger himself flirted with Nazism, a mistake most scholars say he has tragically failed to fully acknowledge. We as human individuals choose from what we are given, commit ourselves to certain traditions and values, shape and alter them to the degree that we can, and pass them on. One can unquestioningly and inauthentically accept the prevailing popular conceptions of culture, or one can actively and authentically seek to carve out one's own unique interpretation of how life ought to be lived. This doesn't mean totally rejecting the offering of history but taking it as a starting point for creative and idiosyncratic departures. The ultimate requirement for doing this is reasonable practical freedom, and the ultimate responsibility is to avoid harm to others and work to expand the freedom of all for authentic pursuits. Heidegger hues more closely to the offerings of history in his discussions of how to live than free-spirited Friedrich Nietzsche who is quick to reject ossified historical traditions and argue for the creation of radically new social practices that serve human creativity.

Let's take a moment to summarize Heidegger's essential position so far. We approach questions of being in the world with an amorphous anxiety and trepidation about our own existential status. Our tendency is to ignore such questions precisely because of the stress they create and trundle on with our lives. On this path, we will never feel quite at home in the world in Heidegger's eyes. To live more authentically and honestly, we need to face up to life's painful realities and in a sense transcend our everydayness by imagining the possibility of nonexistence. This is our ultimate horror, "not-being," and the source of our most obscure but most troubling sense of anxiousness. It's as if we could take a trip out to the edge of some ultimate black hole with the power to suck us up into nothingness and look into its throat. But from such an imagined perspective we can also look back at the universe of our existence, and in doing so what else could we feel but wonder, amazement, astonishment?

Productive and creative acts in Heidegger's eyes originate not just in human endeavors, but start from nature itself. In high mountain meadows when the snow melts in spring, plants emerge from the soil, leaf out to draw energy from the sun, and push forth beautiful flowers to attract bees or hummingbirds that will move pollen from one plant to another thereby activating the reproductive process that will assure a next generation of plants.[12] Human creative activity simply helps along what is already latent in the world of nature. A piece of fine-grained wooden furniture emerges through the work of an artisan from the wood of a large, old tree cut from a forest. Crops spring forth from soils sown by human hand but driven by the energy of the sun. The work of a sculptor unfolds a statue from a large piece of marble created by the forces of nature.[13] The power of the wind turns a windmill

---

[12]The remaining sections in this chapter owe much to the following work: Julian Young, *Heidegger's Later Philosophy* (Cambridge: Cambridge University Press, 2002).

[13]Martin Heidegger, "The Origin of the Work of Art," in *Martin Heidegger: Basic Writings*, ed. David Farrell Krell (San Francisco: Harper, 1992); Martin Heidegger, "The Question Concerning Technology," in *Martin Heidegger: Basic Writings*, ed. David

placed in its path to generate electricity for human use. What human beings do in their everyday working life helps nature along in the creation of objects of utility and value. Humanity and nature act together as partners in an ecological world to create those material objects that satisfy human wants and desires.[14]

Such a naturalized, and some might say romanticized, view of human productive activity on its face has little to do with the reality of the modern industrial society where, with little thought given to nature's creativity, materials ready-to-hand get forcibly extracted from the earth and chemically and mechanically recombined into objects of utility. In the modern industrial world everything becomes strictly a resource, a standing-stock, and this includes human activity. We humans direct the process of cranking out powerful motor vehicles, cell phones, laptops, digital sounds and images, and ready-to-eat fast food, but we also function as cogs in the gears of production. We may feel in control of the assembly system for Ford Explorers or applications for Apple iPads, but in practice the underlying technology is a legacy of a long string of scientific discoveries, engineering achievements, and business practices. At any point in history we are given the technological system available and can tweak it at the margins, but cannot invent it totally anew. In short, we each become but a small piece in a historically given technical and economic system that we are powerless to alter. Now there is nothing wrong with being both an object within and a subject who directs productive activity—after all this is what humans have done in most of their waking hours throughout history. The real issue is whether technology and the economy take over our entire living being, or whether we recognize and enjoy a life and a world beyond the purely material. To cave into the strictly economic in Martin Heidegger's view is to confine oneself to inauthenticity. Instead we should look beyond the current economic horizon to a larger world of natural marvels with an existence of its own to which we owe an obligation of concern and care. The trap of the modern age is a total human absorption in the amazements that modern technology produces

---

Farrell Krell (San Francisco: Harper, 1992).
[14]Martin Heidegger. "Building Dwelling Thinking." In *Martin Heidegger: Basic Writings*, ed. David Farrell Krell (San Francisco: Harper, 1992).

and the ignoring of the even greater amazements that lie beyond the human economic skin. How does one avoid such an entrapment?

The antidote to an inauthentic economic reality is to somehow change our daily work routine to allow us to experience and celebrate the world as a fragile, precious, and wondrous place. Technology needn't be an independent, overpowering force so long as we organize it in such a way as to respect nature's own unfolding and wonders, to see our own actions as the completion of a larger natural process, and to allow our creative impulses to be realized in the production of items and activities not just of utilitarian value, but that connect us to the marvels of Being itself. We all indeed are resources, but we are more than that. We have the privilege of being able to contemplate the world around us and find in it meaning and beauty. The answer to economic and technological dominance is not Luddism, but is to instead transform the economy and technology and render it secondary to the sacredness of existence and beings. One can make use of science and technology without intervening in natural processes for the sole purpose of controlling and exploiting them. Similarly, one can function in the economic arena without disregarding the creative impulses, both natural and human in origin.

Despite such possibilities, technological and economic predominance in our lives is more a matter of fate rather than personal desire according to Heidegger. None of us explicitly chose the economic world we live in. It has simply emerged as a product of the small actions of millions of people over a long span of time. Modernity, where everything is a pure resource and our energies go into endless rounds of producing and consuming, holds sway as a matter of current historical destiny, but this needn't rule out a different future. Treating everything as a pure resource and being stuck on an economic treadmill isn't inevitable.

While we individually lack the capacity for implementing a new economic vision society-wide, we do have a degree of personal choice in the way we live. We can in our daily life move beyond entrapment in consumerism and technology and reintroduce the mystery of Being into our actions. We can individually be "free spirits" who live unconventionally, demonstrating to others the possibility of a personal turning to a new way of being. Eventually, the political weight of those who follow a different vision could be enough to create a larger public move to new arrangements that overcome technological determinism and allow for a more authentic mode of earthly existence. Living one's values in such circumstances inadvertently shapes a larger destiny and could be akin to a communicable virus that can move at lightening speed. The Tunisian and Egyptian revolutions brought forth by "youthful free spirits" attuned to modern communication technology suggests the possibility of a quick and radical turn to a democratic future and away from autocratic rule. How this new movement will pan out remains to be seen, especially in light of Egypt's recent counter-revolutionary coup, but for now fatalism has died in at least one country of the Middle East.

To move beyond a life where the economy holds sway requires something to move towards, which we can discover by expanding our perceptual horizons to take in the idea of dwelling—living in the world in a truly human manner—an idea that Heidegger develops in his later writings.[15] To dwell is to feel safe and cared for in the place where one resides, and to actively care for those others and things that make up this place. To care for something is to passively and actively let it be, to let it unfold itself in accordance with its own nature. In short, we should tune into the wonders of all those beings around us in our dwelling place and extend our care to them as manifestations of the marvels and mystery of existence.

The everyday meaning of the term 'dwelling' is to live in a locality, a place in close proximity to work, schools, shopping and entertainment, friends, and nature's wonders. Dwelling takes on a deeper significance when we do more than just reside in a locality but feel special emotional ties to its environment and way of life. In the presence of such ties, our expressions of care will take form as letting local dwellers seek their self-creative paths through life, a town or city develop according to community needs, architecture fit the aesthetic and natural features of the local landscape, a river follow its own created path, and native flora and fauna play out their evolved natural relationships. To dwell in a

---

[15]Ibid.

deeper sense doesn't mean we forego treating beings as resources—we need resources to live—but to recognize that they possess value and interest in their own right regardless of their resource status.

Dwelling takes more specific form by thinking in terms of the "fourfold": earth, sky, mortals, and divinities (in Heidegger's words). "Earth" and "sky" refer to our natural environment including all its living and nonliving beings and their interconnections. "Mortals" refers not only to our membership as citizens of a larger ecological community, but also to our special presence as self-conscious, thinking, mortal, social beings who have the special capacity to question the meaning of all that we encounter. The final piece of the fourfold, and perhaps the hardest to understand, is the "divinities." One's immediate reaction would be to interpret these as the gods of organized religions, but this is not solely what Heidegger has in mind. Rather, the divine constitutes an unwritten community ethos manifested in the lives of its cultural heroes. Heroes lack divinity in the ordinary religious sense, but they embody in their histories and outlooks values that we hold dear—freedom, justice, courage, care, and generosity. Against our heroes, we judge the content of our own lives. The idea of divinities as framing our lives contains a second more intangible element—an attitude of sacredness towards all beings.

In any lament of the modern condition and its absence of authentic dwelling, technology takes center stage. Technology itself today is encased in a larger economic system fired by constant innovation. The driving force is not just technology, but an extensive media apparatus that entices human consumers to the latest gadgets or symbols of beauty, power, or status created by technological advances. In this arrangement, the powers of technology get directed to stimulating and fulfilling the siren song of consumer craving and satisfaction.

To find authentic meaning and to dwell fully in the world, according to Heidegger's thinking we need to look beyond the horizons created by technology and the economy. To illustrate his meaning, he contrasts the constructing of a bridge and a dam.[16] Building a well-designed bridge to connect two riverbanks and

---

[16]Heidegger, "Building Dwelling Thinking."

their associated landscapes and human communities is an act of dwelling that preserves a river's natural flow and provides a setting that can inspire thoughts of larger connections to humanity and nature, Earth and sky. Building a dam that converts a flowing river into a lake runs counter to authentic dwelling by unnecessarily destroying a natural being. Today we don't need a dam to generate electric energy, but we can do it instead using the blowing wind or the shining sun. One needn't irrevocably harm the processes of nature in the use of it as a resource, nor be a Luddite to save nature's wonders.

To live authentically one must make a concrete choice about the path to follow. Since alternative options from which to choose are already largely established by the forces of history, starting with a clean slate in constructing a life is impossible. Heidegger himself was born into a heritage of conservative rural Catholicism and began his career as a Catholic philosopher, but he soon left the church and sought to broaden his thinking beyond the constraints of religious doctrine. He adopted the language of the philosophical thought of his day, but took it in a sharply new direction. Accepting a particular way of thinking doesn't necessarily mean a rigid adherence to past doctrines. A tradition can serve as a starting point for moving in a new direction as Heidegger demonstrates in his own life as an intellectual.

We all are pushed and shoved about by the contingencies of history, but we can resolutely face up to life's realities and choose that part of our historical inheritance that gives our own life meaning. Much of what we do falls in the realm of the ordinary (Heidegger would say inauthentic as we already noted), but we can still openly choose those values and practices that we judge, on serious reflection, to be especially worthy. Whether this includes elements of a religious tradition is up to us. To select a phenomenon that bears repeating is to adopt a heritage we would want to pass on to the future—the age old rituals of the Catholic Church or the Muslim faith, or perhaps a spiritually oriented environmentalism that sees nature as an amazing and sacred living organism. The choice of an existing tradition does not preclude innovation and creativity in our lives. We can participate in Catholic or Muslim rituals while at the same time advocating for a halt to greenhouse gas emissions, family planning to stabilize global population, or gender equity. To accept a tradition doesn't necessarily mean we have to buy its outmoded details. Nor need we accept prevailing social practices. As post-materialists have discovered, construction of one's own unique spirituality and notion of the sacred remains an open possibility.

Resoluteness is key in making such choices. We can simply go with the flow of popular culture and choose beliefs and practices put forth by others, or we can look carefully at our lives and decide for ourselves what's truly important. A women freely choosing to wear a burqa daily with all but her eyes covered as a sign of faith would be acting resolutely to shape her destiny, but would behave irresolutely if she simply allowed such a practice to be thrust upon her. Nietzsche, the "free spirit," takes an unequivocal position on the question of such choices—when in doubt, get rid of oppressive traditions. Freely choose those that make for a creative life. Heidegger is not so explicit on the standard for choosing what to retain and what to reject.

A heritage for Heidegger is bound up in his notion of divinities.[17] Earth and sky serve as metaphors for the mysteries of nature and the larger universe. World encompasses all the relationships, both cultural and natural, we face as mortal beings. Divinities embody the stories we tell ourselves about the origin and meaning of life and how we should live it. They are the heroes whose lives we choose to emulate. For Heidegger, we psychologically look back to all that we perceive in world from the vantage point of the abyss of "not-being" with both deep anxiety and amazement. From this perspective, we adopt and create traditions and values about how to live. Heidegger infers in us a deep desire to care for beings, but he infers nothing about the existence of God. He is providing a perspective about Being, not a final truth about its content except to say that we all should in some part of our life act as true stewards of the Earth and its occupants.

For any of us moderns who look outside of our personal boundaries towards the world itself for life's meaning, Heidegger is telling us about our need to spiritualize that which gives us feelings of amazement about our existence. To post-materialists having a

---

[17]Ibid.

universalist attachment to both humanity and nature, Heidegger's philosophy directly speaks.

***

Instead of giving special priority to one's bank balance, worry equally, if not more, about having a few good friends, a loving spouse or partner, interesting children with a zest for life, a special passion for work, or art, or sports, or literature, a high regard for free self-expression, tolerance for the beliefs of others, a concern about the well being of both nature and humanity as a whole, and a capacity to enjoy both life's simple pleasures and great wonders. If you hold such an outlook, then you are a post-materialist, one who, in deciding how to live, goes beyond a predominant concern with a security-oriented accumulating of material possessions to a deep appreciation for the qualitative dimensions of life. As a post-materialist, you are also less interested than your elders in organized religion, traditional authority, and patriotism. This doesn't mean you lack spirituality or group commitment, but rather that your values, beliefs, and loyalties orient to the informal and self-created. You may celebrate the wonders of a sunset, but you don't go to church. You are skeptical of hierarchies, but you work passionately in small groups with common goals. And you have trouble seeing military action as the answer for much of anything.

To be clear, post-materialism is an empirical phenomenon revealed in the results of social science research on human values across generational divides. In addressing questions about how to lead one's life, post-materialism exhibits a philosophical tone, but it is not a concept that originated in any direct sense from philosophy as an academic discipline. Most philosophers today worry about the logical structure of language as a means for discovery fundamental truths and don't give a lot of attention to the practical questions of getting through daily life. Of course there are exceptions, and one of the most interesting in my book is Richard Rorty. Rorty's pragmatism directs attention away from questions philosophers have worried about for generations and hones in on issues that arise in coping with the existential contingencies of ordinary life.[18]

---

[18] Richard Rorty, *Philosophy and the Mirror of Nature* (Princeton: Princeton University Press, 1979).

10 Post-Material Philosophy

The conventional philosophical view, that truth is an accurate representation of reality, doesn't get us very far in dealing with the actual problems coughed up by daily being.[18] The really important truths are those beliefs that help us cope, not accurate, objective, and final representations of reality sought by conventional philosophy. You might think an accurate representation of the world just has to be the final test of what is true. Not so, according to Richard Rorty, as we will now see.

Each day I fiddle with the amount of hot water I push through my Aeropress espresso maker, an inexpensive but marvelous device for making good coffee. Too much hot water and the taste becomes bitter, too little and the taste is too strong. What I am looking for is a rough causal relationship between water volume and taste that helps me get a pretty good espresso, a belief that does the job. I could conduct detailed laboratory tests about this relationship had I the requisite skills in experimental chemistry, but I am not sure my taste buds would much notice the resulting difference in my coffee-making skills. I can never be sure how many experiments I would have to run to arrive at a final and accurate representation of the link between hot water volume and espresso taste. How would I ever know when I have arrived at the promised land of final espresso truth? What about controlling for all those other variables, such as water temperature and push time? Is a completely accurate representation worth the cost or even possible? Shouldn't I move on and solve more pressing problems? I haven't even begun to figure out how I could more productively spend my time in my declining years. Is there a final and definitive answer to that question? I doubt it, and the best I can probably do is come up with a few benchmark principles such as keep moving, keep on thinking and writing, keep traveling, do good for someone now and then, and keep marveling at the nature of worldly existence.

To put it simply, what I am claiming here, and what I think Richard Rorty says, is this: Don't bother wasting your time chasing after accurate and final representations of worldly reality. How do you know when you have achieved complete accuracy in a belief that will never need revision? How do you know when you have come to the Nirvana of real truth? For that, there is no test, no final experiment that one can perform. Instead stick with what helps you cope. To have a God's-eye-view perch from which to know the glassy essence of objectivity would be a wonder, but, as trivial as saying so may sound, we reside in the midst of imperfection and ought not to hope for a crystal-clear worldly representation.[19]

If there are no final truths waiting for us to discover, we still have to decide as a society on provisional and pragmatic ones to live by. For many things (and the taste of coffee isn't one of them) we will have little problem finding consensus. The sun we can all agree emerges daily at specific time in a specific place. If we live in Wisconsin, we all agree that the Green Bay Packers are the only football team worthy of our support. But abortion, gun control, and Obamacare present bigger challenges for finding anything near common accord. On Obamacare, the verbal warfare between Democrats and Republicans constitutes what Rorty calls "abnormal discourse."[20] Republicans want to destroy Obamacare, and Democrats want to preserve it at all costs. Were the two sides instead working to iron out differences over, say, the mandate requiring everyone to purchase health insurance, they would be practicing a normal discourse that no longer places them at cross purposes. What we hope for in politics and other arenas of life is an edifying conversation that educates us about new possibilities for dissolving our differences and meeting our common hopes and desires. Most would agree, whether liberal or conservative, that the current discourse on health care is other than edifying.

Among all of society's institutional groupings, scientists seem to have developed the most workable procedure for reconciling different beliefs about how things fit together. The key to doing so is their deep willingness to put hypotheses to the test and accept the results of scientific study and experimentation. Darwinian evolution initially attracted widespread ridicule, but today an overwhelming majority of scientists accept it as the gospel truth in explaining the origins and evolution of life. Scientists give up their deeply held beliefs in the face of good, evidence-based arguments with a greater willingness than many others, as demonstrated in public opinion on global warming. The public at large voices much more skepticism about the reality of greenhouse gas-induced

---

[19]Ibid.; Richard Rorty, *Philosophy and Social Hope* (New York: Penquin, 1999).
[20]Rorty, *Philosophy and the Mirror of Nature*.

climate change than scientists as a group. This doesn't mean the process of arriving at scientific consensus is a pretty one. Scientific disputes rage on for extended periods until edifying discourse kicks in and normalizes the dialogue. Witness the debate on whether the universe is expanding or contracting. Amongst a few scientists, controversy over Darwinian evolution has never gone away, although even here the discord is much greater in the public arena. The special virtue of science is a commitment to a fairly open, balanced, and ultimately edifying dialogue. We just can't know when we have arrived at an accurate representation of reality to justify true and final beliefs. Judgments of our worldly descriptions are by nature a human social act requiring social solidarity with judging others, not reliance on an objective, observation independent reality. If we find our beliefs run against the social grain, we have no choice but to convince others we are right through better arguments. The majority can be wrong and we can be right. For my daily espresso, this doesn't matter; for climate change it does. Scientists have the tough job of convincing the rest of us that we need to take climate change seriously.[21]

In sum, edifying pragmatic philosophers, like Richard Rorty, are suspicious of systematizers who claim to have found a final vocabulary that describes some substantial chunk of reality. Words take their meaning from other words, not as accurate representations of something. Texts and worldly images print little replicas on our retinas. It's up to us to make something of them by relating them to other texts and images and to our various missions that make life worth living. Edifying scientists find new and better theories to describe useful causalities in the material world. Edifying philosophers offer aphorisms, satires, metaphors, and parodies to help us along the path to better descriptions of the cultural landscape we live in, and thinkers more generally do the same with poetry, literature, art, music, drama, or architecture. The key here is inspirations and better beliefs for helping us to understand and cope with the amazing infinity of being. To claim that there are essential and final properties out their waiting to be discovered doesn't really help since we have no way of knowing in

---

[21]Ibid.; Richard Rorty, *Contingency, Irony, and Solidarity* (Cambridge: Cambridge University Press, 1989); Rorty, *Philosophy and Social Hope*.

an infinitely complex, interconnected world when we have arrived at the finality promised land. The task of finding better descriptions is thankfully never-ending. What would we have to do otherwise that's interesting?

Apart from this larger debate about public beliefs, each of us possesses private passions that are nobody else's business. Vincent Van Gogh's deepest desire was to paint simple Provençal rural scenes with unusual coloration and brush strokes. He caused no suffering to others in doing so, and it kept him from losing his sanity earlier than he did. In his life he created a unique capacity for self-expression. After his death, Van Gogh gained high regard for his skills as a painter and a huge, appreciative public following. Many of us are better for having experienced the paintings of Vincent Van Gogh. Whether they become widely known or not, the Van Gogh's of the world should have the opportunity to create their lives as they see fit. Any resulting boons to society at large are serendipitous, but they don't happen if never attempted.

Yet we belong to a social tribe with its public obligations, and in our private lives we all inevitably have public needs. Writers need libraries; artists and art critics need art museums; soccer players need soccer fields; and we all need public education, parks, squares, roads, and transit. We exist both publicly and privately. There is a division, but not so sharp as Rorty seems to think.[22] He limits our public obligation to leaving others alone to pursue their own self-creative purposes and to mitigating human cruelty. Beyond that, our essential duty in his eyes is to diligently pursue our private passions. If anything will serve humanity, it is this. I would say instead, don't neglect your own mission in life, but don't forget you live in a public world. Certainly do what you can to reduce human cruelties, but don't minimize the worth of other public needs including the protection of nature's wonders. The challenge for each of us is to balance our private quests against our public obligations.

We love to explain the shape of our lives to ourselves and others as stories tailored to fit our unique histories. (Think about Bill Clinton and his tales about growing up in Arkansas, or Barack

---

[22]Rorty, *Contingency, Irony, and Solidarity*. This divide is most clearly established in Chapter 4, "Private Irony and Social Hope."

Obama and his struggles as a social worker in Chicago.) In doing this, we all pick and choose from a common set heroes to emulate in our actions and tales, and none of us has the luxury of a perfectly clean slate for shaping and describing how we live. (Clinton liked to model his political life after President John Kennedy.) We begin with the values and purposes endowed us by our background (as Clinton did in his roots as an Arkansas blue dog Democrat), and we start our personal ride from there. Richard Rorty sees us constructing idiosyncratic narratives to shape and explain our lives, and Jean-Paul Sartre, famous existentialist, worries about us letting others determine our lives and narratives for us. People generally don't like to be re-described, and they don't want to be humiliated by someone denigrating their values. (Republicans attempting to embarrass and diminish President Clinton by impeaching him, or Barack Obama by associating him with radical socialism.) Suggestions of new and better values cannot be imposed but must be sold through open conversation and education (Bill Clinton pulling the Democratic Party to the center of the political spectrum, or Barack Obama selling the public on Obamacare). People have to feel as if they are uncovering something better and more truthful themselves. (Democrats buying into Clinton's welfare reforms, or young people signing up on Obamacare exchanges for health insurance.) Whatever we think of the values of others, sneering is not allowed, not even at Republicans. Sneer too much, and we will never make it from abnormal to edifying discourse and political accommodation. Self-creation amounts to inventing one's own self-description and not fully accepting what others say about us. (I.e. a tough grading professor sticking to her guns despite harsh student evaluations.) Find new, more authentic descriptions on your path through life. This is all there is. Take your shots, enjoy the amazing ride, and let eternity take care of itself. Will to self-overcoming; forget about a will to final truth. Yet in our pining for public approval of our private self-creation, there is the danger of caving into popular opinion. (I.e. good student teaching evaluations in exchange for easy grades.) To stick with our idiosyncratic and contingent passions, we may have to forgo public approval. Our social nature causes us to mix up private self-creation and public accommodation in messy ways. Our self-identity is ultimately a private matter, but we always clamor for a public acknowledgement of our private existence. Life is a complicated business.

However we work out our private desires, we have to put up with each other and somehow secure reasonable opportunities for us all. Liberal social hope is a public desire for more freedom, less cruelty, more leisure, and more basic goods, and it is all the social glue we need to justify liberal democracy. Give up on the idea of absolute and final values in support of democracy. Increasing freedom and reducing human and environmental harm is enough justification for liberal democracy for right now, although Republicans at the moment seem to be holding social hope hostage to their radical right wing Tea Party agenda. Of course, by claiming the latter, I may be guilty of pushing abnormal as opposed to edifying discourse.

There is no inference in this that democracy is the perfect solution to our problems. Science and technology have done much in support of social hope and participatory politics, but sadly technology-reliant, rich corporations through lobbying and campaign contributions pervert and redirect democratic politics to their own ends. Corporations as well have done a masterful job of dangling technological, pleasure-bringing toys in front of the consuming masses and turning acts of consumption into superficial sources of meaning, fating much of modern life to get stuck in an economically materialist form where the primary motive is piling up material possessions. The countervailing trend to post-material values pushes back against consumerist meaning, giving priority to the qualitative experiences of life. Instead of becoming technology destroying Luddites, post-materialists embrace technology and shove it towards serving qualitative joys: love, conversation, experiences of wonder, adventures, creations of beauty and understanding, new and novel descriptions, simple pleasures, and so on. With this, I imagine Richard Rorty would be pleased, although he might not like so much my somewhat intolerant attitude towards a majority-supported economic materialism. Post-materialists around the world embrace technologies, such as the Internet and social media, in the service of a more participatory politics, although sometimes with a limited success (i.e. the Egyptian counterrevolution against the Arab Spring). Economic power still runs against the grain of participatory politics, but democracy looks to be the only countervailing option, imperfect as it is. In Richard Rorty's commitment to self-creation, tolerance, freedom, democracy, and cruelty-free human dignity, he counts as a post-materialist, and for this reason his writings should be of interest to all those leading the charge in a new direction. If you are a philosophically inclined post-materialist, give him a look.

***

Philosophical understanding lies in getting to know the details of what philosophers fight about. Philosophy is less about empirical descriptions and more about the presumptions made in thinking about our worldly surroundings. Presumptions matter, but cannot be easily accepted or rejected based on observation alone. These are the things we take on faith to be right, and this is what lies at the root of philosophical differences. Who's right depends on reasoned judgment, not solely on empirical evidence.

Richard Rorty is a pragmatist philosopher who believes the pursuit of objective, final truths to be fruitless and that we should stick to searching for beliefs and ideas helpful in getting us through daily life. Another highly regarded philosopher, Thomas Nagel, claims, in sharp contrast to Rorty, that there is an objective reality discoverable through human inquiry. In a recent work, *Mind and Cosmos,* Nagel runs against the grain of conventional wisdom and argues that human consciousness and thought demands a teleological explanation going beyond conventional theories of evolutionary adaptation.[23] For dyed-in-the-wool pragmatists, myself included, Nagel is a great read for testing out one's basic assumptions about evolution, science, reasoning, and morality.

We humans possess in contrast to other species the special capacity for conscious self-reflection and reason. We own the unique ability to look at our actual and potential beliefs with a critical eye, and to search out those that best fit perceived reality. In doing this we apply our special reasoning abilities to discern and either refine or reject those beliefs that contain a contradiction or incompatibility, or don't fit with our perceptions. While not always successful, we seek to bring accuracy and logical consistency to

---

[23] Thomas Nagel, *Mind and Cosmos: Why the Materialist Neo-Darwinian Conception of Nature Is Almost Certainly False* (Oxford: Oxford University Press, 2012).

our lives in all realms, especially in science, mathematics, and ethics. Our behavior is based both on our inner subjective inclinations and beliefs and outer objectivity whose truth flows from existential reality. Accuracy of representation is what we seek in our interactions with the world beyond our skins. In making the best espresso possible each day, I seek the one best formula for doing so, the final truth about what makes for great espresso. These notions, I think, reasonably reflect Nagel's philosophical outlook.

The truth of the matter is that we have no clue about exactly how consciousness and self-awareness came about in the human species but (apparently) not in others. We humans consciously created mathematics and quantum physics, but other life forms lack such accomplishments insofar as we know. Consciousness of this kind clearly has adaptive advantages, but in terms of normal biological evolution it looks like overkill. To survive and prosper in a hunter/gatherer environment, where human physical evolution did the bulk of its work, self-consciousness, language, and simple reasoning look like good things to have, but the capacity for studying abstract mathematics and the origins of the universe would seem not to be very helpful. In short, human intellectual capacities as they exist look to be a rather fortuitous result of physical evolution. This leads Nagel to conclude that other forces, in addition to simple physical evolution, must play a role in the formation of human consciousness. Nagel also notes the need for an explanation of the formation of life itself, another highly improbable event just like the evolution of human consciousness. We have life but we don't know from whence it came. He sets this more challenging question aside to focus on the emergence of human consciousness and whether biological evolution is enough to explain it.

One can see how the capacity for simple judgment and communication could put evolution on a path to more refined mental activity. "Grunt if you see a lion." This would be marginally adaptive, but could evolve into progressively more complex reasoning and linguistics. More refined grunts can lead to more sophisticated ways of human groups warning about and dealing with threats from lions, and nothing prevents such reasoning abilities to grow in sophistication through cultural evolution and fortuitously takes on a life of its own beyond strict biological need.

The main complaint by Nagel about this explanation is a lack of evidence to back it up. It is a "just so" story, but one that nonetheless has its argumentative attraction. The physical gives us perception of lions and the capacity to grunt, and the mental does the work of putting lion plus grunt together. The physical hardware evolves to take advantage of the software of mental functioning. Biological evolution discovers the advantage of a mental coding system, such as the ones and zeros of modern electronic computers, and puts it to adaptive uses in simple mental reasoning. One for lion, zero for no lion. We cognitively learn from our experiences and perceptions, modify our judgments where prudent in an adaptive fashion. Our life is composed of a series of experiments whose outcomes guide us to better results. The logic of this procedure is a reasonable add-on to the normal evolutionary process. This "just-so" story looks like a serious possibility. A hunter-gather group uses language and causal thinking to work out a better method of hunting big game that advances human fitness. I fiddle with my espresso maker and discover a new way of brewing better coffee. Physicists play with the Hadron Collider and discover what looks to be the Higgs boson. The reasoning process of the modern cosmologist is a logical descendent of that used by the hunter-gatherer.

In Nagel's eyes, sophisticated mental reasoning cannot alone be the result of Darwinian evolution. Not just evolutionary adaptation, but interactions themselves between the mental and physical create the potential for more and more sophisticated mental activity. Complexity begets more complexity and sets the stage for higher level mental functioning. The continuing puzzle is exactly how the complexity of the mental emerges from the physically rooted mental coding system. How do we get from grunts about lions to quantum physics? A possible explanation is that the inherent complexity of the physical system provides a basis for the emergence of the mental. In a sense, the physical already contains roots for the mental in its causal nature. The pre-conscious brain drives and coordinates a body that runs on complex causal relationships. For a non-reductive account of this kind to work, some sort of intrinsic natural teleology, beyond gene-preserving biological adaptive selection, is needed to create self-conscious mental functioning out of the basic physical coding system built into our brains. Given that we rule out the notion of a god-like intentional intervention running the show, what kind of teleology enables us to develop more and more sophisticated patterns of thought beyond the needs of biological adaptation?

Let's accept that human beings have the capacity to form true beliefs about their surrounding world, about the timeless domain of logic and mathematics, and about what to do with their lives. Although not infallible, these capacities can give us objective knowledge according to Nagel. Following the right norms in the acquisition of knowledge, we can gain objective truths about the reality we live in. On their face, these norms of thought go well beyond what's necessary for the usual physical adaptation to naturalistic conditions. If this is the case, how can we understand mind in the fullest sense as a product of nature if nature gives us way more than we need? In short, can our cognitive capacities be placed entirely in a Darwinian framework or need we go further?

For Nagel, evolution alone cannot explain the presence of reason. We use reason to judge accuracy of representation, but the logic of reason is intrinsic and not an evolutionary product. Mathematics, the fact that 2+2=4, has nothing to do with evolution, whereas our dependency on visual and other sorts of perceptions do. Our ability to judge accuracy of representation through reason comes from somewhere else. Basic reasoning grasps truth directly, not through perception. Reason is evolutionarily useful, but stands on its own independent of evolution. Reason has validity in itself. Reason connects us with truth directly; perception connects us with truth indirectly. In ordinary perception, we respond as if using a computer algorithm to establish the specific thing we see. In reason, we understand the logic of the algorithm, how it is truth preserving. Reason allows us to sort out inconsistencies in our apparent perceptions. It serves as a check on whether our perceptions are valid. We have to account for consciousness not only as a perceptive act, but also as a reactive process which double checks whether our immediate conclusions in response to what we observe in the world are right. In doing this we must determine whether there are inconsistencies in what we do, which cases fall under what general principals, and the validity of general principals through experimentation and reasoning. Reason would look to be a development of consciousness independent of any adaptive physical process. Do I kill the good coffee taste by pushing just the right amount of hot water too quickly through the coffee with my Aeropress? Is it generally true that too much water will screw up the coffee? Reason looks to be an independent force that pre-exists in nature, not just in our minds. The physical world runs on general causal laws that obey the rules of reason. How could we humans even gain the capacity to recognize that from incremental physical evolution? This is the mystery that bothers Nagel and causes him to speculate on forces other than evolution alone in the explanation of human mental capacities.

A theory of everything would explain the emergence of living, evolving beings in a lifeless universe, some of whom happen to be self-conscious, and the development of transcendence in those self-conscious beings that allows them to grasp objective reality and value, including scientific conclusions, the eternal truths of mathematics and logic, and objective moral values. We can't rule out reason as a pure fluky side effect of evolution, but a more interesting possibility in Nagel's view is a natural teleology that augments evolution in the creating of a reasoning human consciousness. Given its historical nature, teleology requires an explanation of how a given circumstance evolves from prior conditions. To put it more concisely, some value must exist towards which circumstances will tend. My striving for better coffee is an intrinsic guiding value that drives espresso-production. To do better would require me to acquire ever-more complex and effective espresso machines at considerable expense, something I cannot really afford. My espresso teleology has reached the end of the line; I have reached my feasible coffee Nirvana.

A human value (better espresso; the elimination of poverty; climate stability) originates in either a subjectivist or a realist approach to our worldly interactions. Under a subjectivist account, our dispositional motivations and current beliefs (better espresso brings more pleasure) combine to determine what we see as the right thing to do in a given set of circumstances. I don't want to hit a child crossing a street so I slam on my brakes. A realist account presumes that we seek the right thing to do independent of personal predispositions. We look for what is intrinsically good in the world. I may personally dislike irritating children, but I slam on my brakes because everyone, including children, possesses an inherent right to life (and espresso is inherently good stuff). Just as there are mathematical, physical, and psychological truths out there in the world, there are also moral truths that exist apart from human dispositions.

A Darwinian account of moral value instead originates in fitness-improving moral inclinations that include family commitment, group cooperation, and deterrence of aggression. Other-oriented values conform to an expansive evolutionary account that recognizes adaptive advantages beyond a narrowly conceived self-interested behavior. At a most basic level, we are willing to make deep sacrifices of our own well-being for the sake of those emotionally close to us. Parents are willing to sacrifice their own continuing existence for their children; comrades in arms are willing to die for one another. We also possess varying degrees of empathy and willingness to sacrifice financially for the sake of others not close to us. At Christmas the Salvation Army bell ringers touch our sense of charitable obligation and garner our donations. And finally, we willingly support movements that give us a sense of connection to a larger common purpose or being beyond our personal selves. I donate to environmental groups because of my positive predisposition toward preserving nature today and for posterity. Whatever the source of all such motives, they are dispositional, socially adaptive, and beneficial to group survival. Where else can values come from but within human conscious reflection? How can values formulated in terms of human language come only from without? Interpretation of the perceived world is inevitably driven by the interaction of one's particular dispositions and actual experiences. I look at a tree in terms of its value to me—practically as timber, or environmentally as a living being, or aesthetically as a unique and appealing form, or ecologically as a part of a natural system. For a pragmatist, to talk about independently existing values makes no sense. We come to the world with desires that can't help but shape our outlook towards external being.

But objective realism says that we find values to be intrinsic in the world and not solely a product of biological evolution. Pain is bad because of the traumatic feeling state it induces, but in

Darwinian terms it is also good in its capacity to signal physical harm and stimulate avoidance responses. In realist terms, biologically unnecessary pain is bad in-itself and ought to be minimized where possible. Similarly, a healthy natural world is good because of its intrinsic moral worth. Non-human species populations contain value not just for their additions to human well-being, but also because they possess value in their own right. They have a teleological purpose to perpetuate their kind, a value which functions independently of human presence. A tree possesses an intrinsic value that has nothing to do with my mental inclinations. As a realist, one looks to the ultimate and final form an object takes, its final ideal as an objective being, and whether it possesses intrinsic good or evil.

The big question to which Nagel wants an answer is this: What is a universe like that includes both Darwinian evolution and value realism? In short, on top of the forces of evolution, waiting for our discovery are values with an independent presence beyond our human skins. Objective values come into play in the universe by driving physical systems with natural teleological phenomenon.

Running through this discussion are two visions for philosophy. One spotlights how to better get through the day and to arrange one's life, and the other gives priority to discovering true and final laws of science, reasoning, and morality. The first is pragmatic, the second idealistic and objective. In the first, we begin with our cultural and personal predispositions and seek our path through life recognizing that each of us sees the world somewhat differently, necessitating accommodation with others in our joint endeavors. In the second, accommodation is brought about in the process of discovering the one final truth. When we arrive at a truly objective position, we all end up at the same place. For a pragmatist, our moral values originate in our natural inclinations to advance the well being of our family, our tribe, and our natural home, and are realized with the aid of a reasoning capacity that extends the boundaries of our concerns beyond what is our own to include other beings, human and nonhuman alike, who suffer or face destructive threats. In this way we become progressively more universalistic in our outlook. Moral realism originates in such natural tendencies but takes on an independence of its own with values standing apart from inclinations and accepted for their own sake. The distinction is subtle but important. Values for realists become divorced from Darwinian and cultural evolution. Wherever suffering is found and life of any kind can be fruitfully advanced, moral realism applies independent of personal want. Moral realism becomes the source of teleological value driving human moral actions. Objective values exist apart from individual human beings, are discoverable by all, and are consequently universal in scope. A universalist teleology operates in the arena of human action. Why not in the larger reality outside the human skin and beyond evolutionary adaptation?

We know what biological evolution looks like; consider closely the history of any life form, and one sees evidence of adaptations to physical realities. Beyond culturally rooted human actions, we have no clue how a natural teleology apart from evolutionary adaptation would operate. This simple observation gives one pause in accepting Nagel's vision of a natural teleology distinct from evolution. Where in nature do we find a value-driven teleological system? How, concretely, can a teleological system lead to life itself and to human consciousness? This is a question no one is currently in a position to answer.

In response Nagel would say we haven't discovered new and novel forms of teleology in nature in part because we haven't given much effort to looking. Scientists are too enthralled by evolution to get beyond it. Of course if we look and fail to find anything more than chance occurrence as the inventor of life and consciousness, we haven't really resolved anything. Philosophers will still have something to fight about. Pragmatists and objective realists can still disagree about the fundamental presumptions of philosophy. I will leave the battle to them, although I am personally attracted to the pragmatist view of things. Don't get me wrong. I believe there is a humanity-independent reality out there. If we humans disappeared, I doubt if the universe would much notice and would march on according to its own tune. My only concern is that we humans lack the capacity to attain a human-independent, objective, and complete understanding of that tune. We can nonetheless continue seeking better descriptions of what we think the tune sounds like.

11 Macroeconomics for the Future

Time to descend from the clouds of philosophical speculation, as interesting as they may be, and get back to solving practical problems of earthly being. If our future is indeed post-materialist, we need to worry about how our economy will get unhooked from material consumption as its source of enough economic activity to employ all those who want to work. If anything does, the revival of downtown living symbolizes the post-material form of life to which younger generations increasingly aspire. Downtown living emphasizes shared public experiences in contrast to spatially expansive suburbs oriented to the private accumulation and enjoyment of material possessions. If you live in the suburbs you are more likely to own a spacious dwelling and one or more motor vehicles than if you live downtown. If you live downtown, you are more likely to dwell in a compact apartment or condo and get around on foot, by bike, or on public mass transit than if you live in the suburbs. In short, life in the suburbs encourages entropic consumption, and downtown living facilitates entropically benign experiences. Unsurprisingly, over the last 65 years, the rise of the consumption-oriented suburb has been an essential element in a U.S. consumer-driven economic expansion. Post-materialism suggests a different future that necessarily looks beyond consumption as the dominant force behind macroeconomic demand and employment. To the prospects for this we now turn.

***

In a materialist world where consumption is paramount, a maximal flow of consumer goods distributed over one's lifetime drives economic decision making. For a materialist, the prime desire is for more income and more consumption, and growth in both is a very good thing, and, coincidentally, it's also good for the macroeconomy and employment. More spending at the mall, or another Amazon order, brings both personal pleasure and more income and employment. Added income will be quickly re-injected into the spending stream bringing still further employment increases. Advances in consumer spending are the mother's milk of a high employment economy. Conversely, a collapse in consumer spending brings forth a crashing economy and an explosion in unemployment. To see how this works, lets introduce a few macroeconomic ideas and do a quick review of our most recent economic traumas of the 2007-2009 Great Recession.

To understand the causes of economic decline even at the simplest level, we need to know something about the key measure of our country's economic output, Gross Domestic Product, in shorthand, GDP. GDP measures the total market value of all final goods and services produced within a country's borders in one year. For 2013 in the U.S., this number equals $16,800 billion. Final goods and services are newly produced during the year and end up in the hands of final owners: consumers, businesses for additions to their productive capacity, and governments. The single biggest chunk of output in 2013 went to consumers at 68 percent of total GDP (the absolute dollar amount in this category is symbolized by C). The next biggest category of final goods and services is government (G) at 20 percent in 2013, and following this is private sector investment (I) at 15 percent.[1] The elephant in the room that truly matters for the economy as a whole is clearly consumption.[2]

The Great Recession of 2007 to 2009 has its roots in a housing market boom that began in the early 2000s and culminated with a crash in housing demand and plunging housing prices in 2007. Between 2007 and 2009, the economy shed 8.5 million jobs and the unemployment rate rose from 4.7 to 10.1 percent. In comparison to a long-term trend line, consumer spending in 2011 stood $7,300 per person below what it otherwise would have been had the recession not occurred.[3] Of the total jobs lost, about a third can be attributed to the decline in consumption, and most of the rest to a precipitous drop in investment spending.[4] Whenever the

---

[1] A part of investment spending (I) goes towards the purchase of newly constructed housing. Even though households are the final buyers of new residential dwellings, new housing is counted in I, not consumption C. At the tail end of the list of GDP components is net exports (X), and it comes in for 2013 at a negative 3 percent because we import more than we export.

[2] U.S. Council of Economic Advisors, "Economic Report of the President, 2014," (Washington D.C.: U.S. Government Printing Office, 2014).

[3] Kevin J. Lansing, "Gauging the Impact of the Great Recession," *FRBSF Economic Letter*, no. 2011-21 (2011).

[4] U.S. Bureau of Labor Statistics, "Consumer Spending and U.S. Employment from the

economy as a whole slows down, businesses immediately cut their spending on additions to their capital plant and inventories. Businesses add productive capacity whenever more sales are expected, but the rug will be quickly removed from such expectations by a financial panic and economic decline, and this is exactly what happened in 2007 and 2008. The real culprit in getting the economic ball rapidly rolling downhill was residential housing construction specifically, and reduced spending related to the housing market generally. From its peak in 2005, residential construction declined from $856 billion and 34 percent of investment spending down to $392 billion and 21 percent in 2009.[5] Historically in recessions, households move slowly in cutting back spending, but special circumstances prevailed in 2007-2008 that sent consumer goods purchases tumbling. To this issue we now turn.

The bursting of a housing bubble in 2006 in combination with a highly speculative and fragile financial system set the stage for a rapid dive into recession starting in late 2007. From 2001 on, low interest rates, unusually lax mortgage lending standards, and the creation of subprime loan instruments that extended homeownership to families who don't ordinarily qualify for conventional mortgages brought about a boom in both new housing construction and purchases of existing housing, driving housing prices rapidly upwards.[6] A housing boom functions through a contagion of optimism characteristic of financial booms generally, the nature of which Robert Shiller convincingly describes in his book, *Irrational Exuberance*.[7] A desire to get on the bandwagon of rising prices fueled growth in the homeownership rate to a new high by 2006. Homeowners took advantage of rising values by getting their hands on huge amounts of spendable cash through mortgage refinancing at low rates and home equity loans, and much of this new cash went to funding a

---

2007-2009 Recession through 2022," *Monthly Labor Review* (2014), http://www.bls.gov/opub/mlr/2014/article/consumer-spending-and-us-employment-from-the-recession-through-2022.htm.

[5] U.S. Council of Economic Advisors, "Economic Report of the President, 2014."
[6] Lansing, "Gauging the Impact of the Great Recession."
[7] Robert J. Shiller, *Irrational Exuberance*, Second ed. (Princeton: Princeton University Press, 2005).

boom in consumer purchases. A rise in housing values well above historical norms couldn't last, and prices came tumbling down dramatically reducing household wealth and driving many homeowners underwater with home values falling below outstanding mortgages. Unsurprisingly, mortgage defaults accelerated, a story that is familiar to us all. With a drastic decline in the worth of their most valuable asset, their house, and extraordinary debt obligations, consumers had little choice but to curtail their spending. With the slowing of the economy, businesses began laying off workers in the face of shrinking product demand and cut back on investment spending leading to further layoffs in the construction and capital goods industries. Needless to say, new housing construction dropped precipitously putting a huge dent in construction employment. The economy probably could have recovered from the drop in new housing construction,[8] but once housing value declines took hold and home loan defaults began to rise, the writing was on the wall.

The tale of financial market woes following the housing market crash is complex in its details but conceptually fairly simple. From the early 2000s on, financial institutions packaged mortgage loans together into securities in increasingly novel and innovative ways, and sold them to investors to the tune of trillions of dollars. Unbeknownst to investors, many of these securities were at high risk for default even though rating agencies put a low-risk stamp of approval on them. At the same time, a huge array of other financial instruments, many based on fragile pyramids of underlying asset valuations, were also being created. In short, with the bursting of the housing market, this whole system of newfangled financial instruments came tumbling down, stock markets around the world plunged, and a number of U.S. financial institutions had to be bailed out by the Federal Reserve to save the economy from a free fall.[9]

---

[8] Paul Krugman, *End this Depression Now!* (New York: W.W. Norton, 2012).

[9] As you can imagine a huge literature has emerged on the financial roots of the Great Recession. For an elegantly simple summary, see Chapters 7-9, Paul Krugman, *The Return of Depression Economics and the Crisis of 2008* (New York: W.W. Norton, 2009). For a detailed look at the role economic bubbles play in financial and housing markets see Shiller's, *Irrational Exuberance* and *The Subprime Solution: How Today's Global Financial Crisis Happened and What to Do about it* (Princeton: Princeton University Press, 2008).

Not only did the U.S. Federal Reserve undertake unprecedented financial rescue measures from 2007 to the present day to save the economy from economic depression, but the Obama Administration and Congress put into effect an economic stimulus plan amounting to nearly $900 billion dollars.[10] Without this and other government measures to stabilize and stimulate the economy, no doubt we today would be referring to the Great Recession as the Second Great Depression. In the 1930s Great Depression, Keynesian economics was born only to fall out of favor in recent decades, but has now regained traction in the political arena, except of course among staunch, small government conservatives. During recessions, depressions, and financial panics, consumers and businesses withdraw spending from economic circulation, bringing on economic decline and rising unemployment. This was the simple insight of John Maynard Keynes, and it brought him to conclude that in depressions and recessions government will be the only institution left standing with the power to replace lost spending and recharge the demand for goods and services. The historical proof for this is wartime military spending in the 1940s that finally brought an end to the Great Depression of the 1930s. The Obama Administration in the American Recovery and Reinvestment Act of 2009 instituted government spending increases and tax reductions to stimulate the economy including new infrastructure projects, transfers to budget strapped state and local governments, boosts in assistance to the unemployed, and a social security tax holiday and other tax cuts. One estimate finds that this effort increased jobs by 2.7 million workers and cut unemployment by 1.5 percentage points.[11] The usual complaint with fiscal policy of this sort is its deficit financing, but without a concerted fiscal and financial effort to turn the economy around, economic decline would have caused the deficit to increase by much more than it actually did.

---

[10] Mark Zandi and Alan S. Blinder, "How the Great Recession was Brought to an End," (West Chester, PA: Moody's Analytics, 2010). For a less charitable view of the sufficiency of the Obama Administration's economic stimulus efforts and a full take on our current economic crisis, see Krugman, *End this Depression Now!* For a similar view, see Joseph E. Stiglitz, *Freefall: America, Free Markets, and the Sinking of the World Economy* (New York: W.W. Norton, 2010).
[11] Zandi and Blinder, "How the Great Recession was Brought to an End."

The essential thought I hope to leave you with here is this: government spending and tax measures can be brought into the breach where private sector spending is not up to the task of employing all those who want to work.

***

For post-materialists consumption is important, but only insofar as it serves the experience of life. This infers an upper limit on lifetime consumption and income flows, above which more interferes with desired life experiences. One needs time and the opportunity to smell the roses, and many of those roses lay outside the arena of private consumption. To the materially satisfied, another day at the park, riding one's bike, or reading a book at the library will look better than work or shopping. For post-materialists, income increases will just pile up in savings rather than go to spending. For materialists, some portion of any income increase will instead be devoted to expanding consumption. These two behavioral regimes will have vastly differing effects on the country's macroeconomic performance.

To get a clear picture of why this is so, let's begin with a simple but extreme case where we all convert to post-materialism in one fell swoop and achieve our desired upper limit on consumer spending right away. In a materialist world we were all happy to expand our acquisition of material goods along with growth of our incomes over time, but now we have lost interest in this and prefer to spend our time in other pursuits. As we described above, the economy as a whole is composed of three basic sectors responsible for spending on newly produced goods and services: consumption, investment, and government.[12] Consumption is the elephant in the room at around 65 percent of the total pie, so if it suddenly stops growing, it truly matters. To keep the story from getting too complicated, let's take population and the labor force to be stable, meaning that growth in the supply of real (inflation adjusted) GDP comes entirely from labor productivity[13] improvements that flow from various sources including better education and job training, more capital goods such as computers and manufacturing robotics, and more efficient technologies. If productivity grows by 1 percent

---

[12]Net exports, the fourth component, is small enough for us to ignore.
[13]Labor productivity equals real GDP per hour worked.

a year, this means we all have to spend 1 percent more or else we won't have bought everything our economy can produce nor have fully employed all its resources, labor in particular, and unemployment will rise. In short, the spending treadmill needs to speed up each year by the rate of productivity improvement, or else we won't need as many total hours of employment. Spending less than an added 1 percent will bring either layoffs or per employee reductions in hours worked, and in the U.S. businesses reduce total hours of employment mostly with layoffs. In a materialist world, labor and capital incomes rise along with productivity and flow to added consumer spending. In a post-materialist world, incomes rise along with productivity, but if spending remains stable, unspent income increases land in savings, unsold goods pile up, and layoffs result.

Productivity growth is a good deal if we are all materialists and increase spending as our incomes grow, but not so good if we are post-materialists and direct added income flows entirely to savings. In the later instance, unemployment will chronically rise if nothing is done. Take heart, we can remedy the problem, although you might not like the fix if you are a small government conservative.

We have two obvious solutions to perpetually rising unemployment caused by a combination of labor productivity growth and stable consumption: (1) shift the responsibility for growth in macroeconomic demand from consumption to government, or (2) eliminate layoffs as the means to adjust total work hours downward and instead give everyone shorter hours and more leisure, or what I call the "European" solution. Let's begin with demand growth shifting.

You might be wondering why we don't consider increased growth in private sector investment spending as part of the answer to consumer spending stagnation, but the rigidity of linkages between consumption and investment complicates this option. The essential task of business investment in a consumption-dominated economy is to fund capital goods, such as machines, computers, buildings, and other long-lived items, needed for the production of consumer goods. Such business investment is undertaken for essentially two purposes: to replace used-up and obsolete capital goods with new, and to add to the economy's capacity to produce more stuff. Simply put, replacement investment depends on the current size of the consumer goods sector while capacity-expanding investment turns on the amount of that sector's anticipated growth. Replacement investment hinges on the rate of capital goods wear and tear and obsolescence, which in turn will bear a relationship to the total capital stock required for current consumer goods production. New investment instead depends on the amount of growth in the consumer goods sector, and less growth in consumption will thus mean an absolute decline in investment spending. Investment spending is the tail that is wagged by the consumer spending elephant, and for this reason we need to look elsewhere for a replacement growth engine.

All this really leaves is government for the task of offsetting stagnating growth in consumer spending.[14] Let's put some numbers on consumption and government spending for a more concrete picture of how government spending can be altered to take care of a slowdown in consumer spending growth and put it all in per capita and real terms to eliminate population growth and inflation from complicating the story.[15]

From 2000 to 2013, U.S. inflation adjusted (real) GDP per capita grew from $44,600 to $49,900, a growth rate of a little less than 1% annually. At the same time, real per capita consumer spending grew at a little more than 1% per year, ending up at $33,900 in 2013, and real per capita government spending reached $9,200 after growing at an anemic .3% per year. The share of consumption in total GDP currently equals 67% and the same number for government is 20%, meaning that consumption contributes more than three times as much as government (3.35 to be exact). In other words, to offset a reduction in the growth of consumer spending of 1%, the growth rate of government expenditures would need to increase from its current .3% to 3.65% or an addition of 3.35%, not a happy prospect for anyone who wants to see government shrink instead. In short, to keep the economy growing, government spending will need to expand

---

[14]The only other component of GDP is net exports, but it is too small to generate much growth.
[15]We have to be careful in defining the meaning of government spending here. In GDP accounting, government expenditures G refers to spending on goods and services, i.e. bombs, roads, and park rangers, not on transfer payments such as Social Security checks for the retired.

enough to offset the declining consumption growth brought on by parsimonious post-materialists.

Post-materialists will probably be perfectly happy with added government spending going to fund public goods that support shared public experiences and government actions that advance personal autonomy and environmental improvement. Pragmatic government action to solve problems of the day is a good thing in post-materialist eyes so long as basic self-expressive freedoms don't get trumped in the process. But a 3.65% growth rate in government spending on goods and services annually may not appeal to everyone, especially post-materialists with libertarian leanings. Over the very long haul, government would eventually become the dominant sector in the economy doubling in size about every twenty years. While post-materialists might be happy to see per capita spending increase on life-enhancing public goods, they may not be too excited about government becoming the dominant force in the economy. We do have to remember we are considering an extreme case. Rather than all of us, perhaps as many as a fourth of us might be post-materialists in say 20 years with the rest of us remaining on a materialist path. This would cut back on the amount of government spending growth we would need to sustain full employment, but the principle would remain the same. Government would still need to expand in relative terms to offset slower growth in consumption.

As we will now see, a huge growth in government can be avoided by instead following the so-called "European" solution. If we in the U.S. follow the recent European experience, we would use increased labor productivity to pay for work hours reductions and expanded leisure rather than consumer spending. The essence of the idea is to take advantage of greater productivity by keeping aggregate incomes stable and working fewer hours while still producing a fixed bundle of consumer goods for each of us. Sounds like nirvana to me, although I may like leisure more than some.

If we go back to the 1970s, the average weekly hours worked per employed person in the U.S. and Western Europe were roughly equal. By 2004, workers in Italy, France, and Germany respectively put in 8, 7, and 6 hours less per week than those in the U.S. The primary reason for these lower average hours is an increase in legally mandated and negotiated vacation days, sick leave, and holidays in Europe, resulting in Europeans working substantially less than they did in 1970, while Americans continued putting in about the same amount of weekly hours.[16] Europeans have taken some of their addition in hourly wages in recent decades in the form of leisure, but Americans have chosen to focus on increasing their take home pay instead. Why this has happened is an interesting puzzle,[17] but the feasibility of reducing hours in a modern affluent economy is what concerns us here. If our consumption practices become increasingly post-materialist in this country, or anywhere else, then reducing average weekly hours is a simple and painless way to adjust an economy's aggregate output to a lessened aggregate demand without killing off the employment goose that lays the economic golden egg. Instead of layoffs to adjust to demand growing more slowly than supply, we all cut our total hours of work to match our productivity increases. If we are more productive to the tune of say 1% a year, then we cut our hours to the same tune.

Employers who resist cutting hours but instead cut people constitute the one barrier to this strategy. In the U.S. especially, employers find it more profitable to cut people instead of hours per person primarily because doing so can reduce the fixed cost of health insurance benefits associated with people. For Europeans, this is not an issue because health care or insurance is provided and paid for publicly outside of employment whereas in the U.S. many receive their health insurance as an employee benefit. The recently passed Affordable Health Care Act (Obamacare) moves the U.S. away from an employment-based health insurance system and reduces the associated business cost-savings from cutting people. In the future, employers will more likely offer cash health care benefits proportionate to wage rates and encourage employees to privately purchase their insurance on state exchanges. Some predict the final result will be a move to a lower cost, single payer,

---

[16]Alberto Alesina, Edward Glaeser, and Bruce Sacerdote, "Work and Leisure in the United States and Europe: Why So Different?," in *NBER Macroeconomics Annual 2005*, ed. Mark Gertler and Kenneth Rogoff (Cambridge: MIT Press, 2005).
[17]Adam Okulicz-Kozaryn, "Europeans Work to Live and Americans Live to Work (Who is Happy to Work More: Americans or Europeans," *Journal of Happiness Studies* 12(2011).

Medicare-like health insurance system. Once this happens, health insurance will be completely divorced from employment and the benefit from cutting people as opposed to hours per employee will have gone away.[18]

Cutting hours as opposed to people looks like a good strategy for adapting to a post-materialist world. If the Europeans can do it, so can we.[19] If you don't like the idea of expanding the role of government in the economy to offset unemployment from slower growth in consumer demand, then you may like having to work less as a macroeconomic strategy instead.

---

[18] A similar problem exists with employer-born employee training costs. By hiring fewer people, U.S. businesses avoid fixed job training costs much as they do for health insurance. Again, this problem largely goes away in Europe where more employment training is publicly funded than in the U.S.

[19] The Netherlands offers one of the best models for cutting hours. See A. Hayden, "Work-time Reduction and the Dutch Economic Miracle," (Toronto: 32 Hours: Action for Full Employment, 1999); Jelle Visser, "The first part-time economy in the world: a model to be followed?," *Journal of European Social Policy* 12, no. 1 (2002).

12 Economic Democracy

Judging from the positive response to Thomas Piketty's now famous *Capital in the Twenty-First Century*, many now agree that a defining and damaging feature of the global economy today is an extreme inequality of capital ownership.[1] A means for reducing such inequality mentioned by Piketty is a democratization of wealth ownership that extends more widely the opportunity to become full-fledged capitalists. Instead of pursuing this line of reasoning, Piketty focuses on a global wealth tax as a more realistic strategy for mitigating economic inequality, but in doing so he just might be selling short capital democratization. Perhaps he avoids this approach on grounds that it is too radical to be of practical importance, but a tried and true method compatible with modern economic arrangements is available—expanding the participation of employees in the ownership and governance of businesses for which they work. If employees become substantial owners of capital, then wealth automatically de-concentrates, bringing down economic inequality.

Employee ownership and control not only matters for the inequality of income received from business profits, but also for the relative distribution within an enterprise of income from wages and salaries. An employee owned and controlled enterprise turns the hiring decision on its head. Instead of management hiring labor, labor now hires management and can directly control income inequality by establishing maximum ratios between the earnings of the highest and lowest paid positions within the business. The modern phenomenon of manager-controlled boards setting top management compensation at extraordinary levels now disappears. Democratically elected, employee controlled boards can set internal maximum income ratios between the highest and lowest pay scale at the minimum necessary to attract managers with the appropriate skills to run the show. In short, managers under employee ownership lose the power to set their own rates of compensation. Managerial marginal product, the actual addition

---

[1] Thomas Piketty, *Capital in the Twenty-First Century* (Cambridge: Harvard University Press, 2014).

they make to the bottom line, would rule the day in setting compensation, not managerial political power.

Under employee democracy, workers would also be able to influence organization decisions on the normal workweek, overtime, vacations, and the organization of work itself, constrained, of course, by the requirements of competition in the larger economy. These features post-materialists will find appealing on the job, since they place freedom of expression and having a say at work ahead of economic growth as essential social goals. Millennials, many who subscribe to post-material values, more than others desire to have frequent feedback on both their own employment performance and how their work fits into their employer's larger organizational strategy.[2] Millennials also express a greater willingness than others to sacrifice income for meaningful work that has a positive social impact. They want the work they do to matter. A study by The Intelligence Group reports that 64 percent of Millennials would rather earn $40,000 a year at a job they love than $100,000 a year at a job they find unfulfilling. The Intelligence Group's Jamie Gutfreund studies generational trends and differences, and she finds that "Millennials were raised with a different perspective."[3] They desire their employer to help make the world a better place and they want to contribute to those efforts, and one path to achieving this goal is through employee democratic representation.

Conventional businesses run on top-down authority as opposed to a bottom-up democratic form of decision-making, and their fundamental drive is to maximize profits and shareholder value instead of achieving broader social goals such as economic equity or democratic participation. Post-materialist values as a consequence get short shrift. A reasonable path to fulfilling both the desire for democratic participation and economic equity is a relative expansion of employee ownership in the economy as a

---

[2]Jessica Brack, "Maximizing Millennials in the Workplace," (Chapel Hill UNC Kenan-Flagler Business School, 2014); Center for Women and Business, "Millennials in the Workplace," (Waltham, MA: Center for Women and Business, Bentley University, 2012).
[3]Rob Asghar, "What Millennials Want in the Workplace (And Why You Should Start Giving it to Them)," Forbes, http://www.forbes.com/sites/robasghar/2014/01/13/what-millennials-want-in-the-workplace-and-why-you-should-start-giving-it-to-them/.

whole. To be certain that this is indeed the case, we need to look in more detail at the feasibility of employee ownership as a form of business organization and how its expansion can occur.

***

The most famous and studied example of employee ownership is an extensive system of producer cooperatives centered in Mondragon, a town of 22,000 located in the mountainous Basque region of Spain. Founded in 1956 by 25 workers educated together at a local technical school, the first Mondragon cooperative has grown into a federated system, known as the Mondragon Cooperatives Corporation, composed of 289 companies employing some 80,000 throughout Spain in manufacturing, retailing, finance, and education. Central to Mondragon's success is a large, credit cooperative, the Caja Laboral, that today operates over 400 local branches. The Caja, a jointly owned second degree cooperative, greases the financial skids of growth for the system as a whole and fosters the creation of new enterprises through its Empresarial division by seeking out and assisting workers desiring to start new cooperatives. A close second in importance for the success of the larger system are a number of educational cooperatives, including the Mondragon University, that pair academic instruction with extensive technical training. Critical also to economic achievement are Mondragon's technology research centers that currently hold more than 500 patents and help to keep individual manufacturing cooperatives abreast of the latest innovations in their respective industries. At the economic foundation of the cooperative system is its industrial sector producing an array of home appliances, furniture, sporting goods, motor vehicle components, and capital goods. Second in importance to manufacturing is Mondragon's Eroski retail group and its 2,400 stores in Spain and southern France, including super markets, travel agencies, petrol stations, and perfume and sporting goods stores.[4]

Mondragon differs fundamentally from a conventional corporation in its ownership and governance structure. Employees,

---

[4]For an important early description and analysis of Mondragon, see Henk Thomas and Chris Logan, *Mondragon: An Economic Analysis* (London: Allen and Unwin, 1982). For a recent evaluation of Mondragon, see Saioa Arando et al., "Assessing Mondragon: Stability & Managed Change in the Face of Globalization," (Ann Arbor: The William Davidson Institute, 2010).

not stockholders, own each cooperative and through membership in a general assembly elect its management committee. The committee in turn hires managers and oversees their performance. On becoming a member, each employee purchases a share in the cooperative, usually financing it with a loan paid back through a payroll deduction. Each year, a tenth of a cooperative's profits go to charitable activities in the local community, twenty percent ends up in a rainy day reserve fund, and the rest is distributed to individual employee-owner interest bearing capital accounts that can be withdrawn only on retiring or resigning from the cooperative. These retained funds, normally deposited with the credit cooperative, Caja, provide a key source of finance for new capital plant purchases and other investments by any cooperative in the system as a whole. In short, labor hires and controls capital, turning conventional capitalism on its head, making a big difference in both the work experience and distribution of income and wealth. Each employee has a say in the running of the business through the power of their vote and interactions with management committee representatives, and each shares in the business's surplus earnings through their ownership share.

Economic inequality within each Mondragon cooperative is directly controlled by a ceiling on the ratio of the highest to lowest base pay over all employment positions. In the early days, the ceiling was set no greater than 3 to 1, meaning that pay for the top manager in a cooperative could be no more than three times that for the lowest paid position. In recent years, to attract good managers, the official ratio has risen to 9 to 1 for some cooperatives.[5] This ratio also plays a role in the determination of annual profit distributions to individual capital accounts since relative amounts are based on each member's total annual wage payment. Capitalist corporations rarely make any attempt to explicitly control internal economic inequality; in cooperatives operating on Mondragon principles, internal inequality is under democratic control, and an increase in inequality occurs only if it benefits the organization as a whole. Thomas Piketty's concern for the tendency of inequality to rise in a capitalist economic system would be greatly dampened were cooperatives to become a

---

[5]Ibid.

substantial portion of the total economy. A special bonus for post-materialists from a cooperative economy would be satisfaction of their desire for more say on the job.

If in comparison to capitalist enterprises, cooperatives possessed a lower rate of productive efficiency or a lesser capacity to withstand competitive pressures, their participatory virtues would be trumped by threats to their ultimate survival in the global marketplace. The five-decades of survival and growth of Mondragon offers strong evidence for the capacity of a cooperative system to experience long-term economic health and prosperity. Comparative studies find that Mondragon cooperatives exhibit greater productive efficiency than their capitalist counterparts and greater rates of growth in output and employment. Their array of supporting institutions for education, research, entrepreneurial support, and finance appear to give Mondragon cooperatives a special advantage compared to their capitalist competition in both productivity and innovation. Perhaps most important of all in Mondragon's success is its participatory structure creating a kind of "moral bond" between individual employee members and their organization that drives a constant quest for finding better ways of doing business.[6]

Given its competitive advantages over the conventional businesses, the lack of a more expansive global cooperative economic sector looks puzzling at first glance. The essential barrier to the creation of a cooperative economy turns out to be the rare conditions required for its initial formation. Once a cooperative system is established it can be self-perpetuating as the Mondragon experience suggests. Individual new cooperatives can be established within a larger system by way of internal schemes of support for entrepreneurs with ideas and plans for new ventures. The problem comes in establishing the cooperative system itself. Mondragon's founding cooperative guru was Don Jose Maria Arizmendi, a local parish priest. Using his knowledge of economics, cooperative history, and Catholic social teaching, Don Jose sought to bring back prosperity to the local Basque economy, gravely damaged in the Spanish Civil War, by establishing a technical school for training the young in industrial skills and the

---

[6]Ibid. Also see Thomas and Logan, *Mondragon: An Economic Analysis*.

principles of cooperation. Graduates soon founded the first cooperative for the production of cook stoves, and Don Jose spearheaded the formation of a credit cooperative to help fund local development. Today we would call Father Arizmendi and his students "social entrepreneurs," individuals who establish business organizations for both the achievement of a social purpose and the earning of an income. The social purpose of Mondragon is to advance economic prosperity for everyone in the Basque region of Spain as well as to promote the principles of social and economic cooperation. In the context of a profit driven global capitalist system, social entrepreneurship looks like a fairly rare phenomenon, but we will see later that such may not be the case looking into the future.[7]

Sticking with "idealistic social values" for a huge organization such as Mondragon in an intensely competitive global economy can be a serious challenge. A Mondragon enterprise, as any cooperative, faces the danger of "degeneration" through the replacement of older members who retire with less costly nonmembers who don't share in governance or profits. This strategy in its rawest sense amounts to exploitation of nonmember employees by a cooperative's members. By hiring outsiders, each member will gain a larger piece of the profit pie in a shrinking pool of full cooperative participants. To prevent such degeneration within Mondragon, in the 1990s all industrial cooperatives located within Spain established a target of at least 85 percent member employment, and currently 89 percent of industrial cooperative employees are also full-fledged members.

Outside the Spanish industrial cooperatives, Mondragon still faces hurdles in achieving its membership goals and preventing its transformation to a conventional form of businesses organization. The largest numbers of nonmember Mondragon employees are found in the Eroski retail group and in Mondragon-owned Chinese subsidiaries. Facing competitive challenges from other retail chains, Eroski undertook a strategy of rapid expansion in Spain and France outside the Basque region beginning in the 1980s through both new store construction and acquisitions. Expanding the cooperative form of ownership to 30,000 new employees

---

[7]Ibid.

would have been too cumbersome to accomplish quickly, and the more flexible conventional labor contract was adopted instead to facilitate rapid growth. In the meantime, a voluntary partial ownership program has been established and extended to some 5,000 additional employees on top of the 9,000 that are already full employee-owners, and a plan is now in place to bring all 50,000 Eroski employees under the full cooperative ownership umbrella.

Mondragon, like conventional businesses around the world, had little choice but to meet the challenges of economic globalization, and it did so by creating overseas subsidiaries to gain access to foreign markets and to counter the threat of competitors moving plants to countries with low labor costs. Mondragon currently employs about 12,000 non-owning workers in its Chinese subsidiaries serving both domestic and export markets. The ultimate goal of overseas expansion is less to expand cooperative ownership abroad than it is to sustain employment in cooperatives at home in complementary activities. Whether Mondragon can extend its cooperative model overseas remains an open question. The Chinese, despite their collective economic experiences of the past, lack familiarity with the ideas of employee ownership, profit sharing, and democratic participation in management. Nonetheless, Mondragon plans to begin introducing such ideas to its Chinese employees and experimenting with partial ownership plans. Whether this effort can succeed remains an open question.[8]

Creating a cooperative economy subscribing to those principles followed by Mondragon remains a substantial challenge, but doing so would better serve post-materialist values than the capitalist alternative, as we have already argued. The essential dynamic for creating a capitalist enterprise is the ability for a founding entrepreneur to lay claim to present and future profits generated by the business. This is the reward for gambling one's savings, time, and energy on a new business venture. In creating a cooperative

---

[8] Arando et al., "Assessing Mondragon: Stability & Managed Change in the Face of Globalization." Also, see Anjel Errasti, "Mondragon's Chinese Subsidiaries: Coopitalist Multinationals in Practice," *Economic and Industrial Democracy* Forthcoming (published online eid.sagepub.com)(2013); Anjel Errasti et al., "The Internationalisation of Cooperatives: The Case of the Mondragon Cooperative Corporation," *Annals of Public and Cooperative Economics* 74, no. 4 (2003).

enterprise, the founders will own an equal share of the business along with all other employee-members, and perhaps win access to somewhat higher paid managerial positions, but even that is not assured given the democratic process underlying the selection of managers. Social motives will need to stand beside economic drives for the establishment of cooperatives. Once a cooperative system on the order of Mondragon comes into being, the risk of founding new enterprises can be substantially reduced through a support system offering venture finance, technical assistance, and trained employees, but strong social motive will still be required for the founding of the system itself. Without Father Don Jose Maria Arizmendi's selfless efforts in the initial founding of Mondragon, it would likely not exist today. Creating employee-owned enterprises in the first place is the essential challenge, but it just may be overcome by the emergence of post-materialist values driving a global expansion in social entrepreneurship as we will now argue.

***

Making as much profit as possible defines the essential drive of a capitalist and materialist economy. Only those economic innovations that bring significant profits will be of interest to materialistic capitalists. In a post-materialist world, the motivation for innovation broadens. Profitability continues to be important, but innovation takes on a social dimension as well. Post-materialist innovators possess a broader array of social goals in the work that they do than profit alone. We get a hint of this in the Sergey Brin and Larry Page experience of founding Google. They went into business because they wanted to create the best possible Internet search engine.[9] Of course they made an incredible amount of money along the way making the attainment of their social ends a whole lot easier and more pleasant.

The idea of social innovation has gained a special currency among academic researchers in recent years seeking to understand the driving forces behind what has come to be known as "social entrepreneurship." The notion of "entrepreneurship" has been around for a very long time and refers to the act of creating and running a new business that delivers a good or a service for the

---

[9]Edwards, *I'm Feeling Lucky: The Confessions of Google Employee Number 59.*

purpose of making a profit. "Social entrepreneurship" refers instead to the act of creating and running a new organization with a goal of accomplishing a social purpose as well as making a profit. Both the founders of Google and Facebook have publicly expressed social goals for their organizations alongside achieving a threshold of profitability.

Survey researchers work to identify concretely the phenomenon of social entrepreneurship with a question that takes the following form: "Are you, alone or with others, currently trying to start or currently owning and managing any kind of activity, organization or initiative that has a particularly social, environmental or community objective?" A second question ascertains whether a survey respondent is involved in starting a for profit enterprise: "Are you, alone or with others, currently trying to start a new business or owning and managing a company, including any self-employment or selling any goods or services to others?" Respondents answering the first question positively are "social entrepreneurs" while respondents answering the second question positively are "commercial entrepreneurs." In cases where the same respondent reports a positive response to both questions, a third question is asked to determine if the businesses referred to in the two responses are one in the same, and if so the overlapped enterprise counts as a social business. Across an adult population survey sample of from 49 countries at different stages of economic development, the incidence of early stage social entrepreneurialism (an organization that is 3.5 years old or less) ranges from a high of 4.1 percent in the United Arab Emirates to a low of .1 percent in Guatemala. The rate for the U.S. is comparatively high at 3.9 percent. The global average is 1.8 percent with low-income countries averaging 1.3 percent, middle income 1.8 percent, and high-income countries 1.9 percent. The incidence of total early state entrepreneurialism for all countries, including both social and pure commercial, averages 10.7 percent with the respective figures for low, middle, and high income countries equaling 16.9, 11.3, and 6.6.[10]

---

[10]Brigitte Hoogendoorn and Chantal Hartog, "Prevalence and Determinants of Social Entrepreneurshp at the Macro-level," in *EIM Research Reports* (Zoetermeer: Panteia/EIM, 2011).

Given what we know about post-materialist and materialist human motivations, we would expect post-materialists to be attracted with greater frequency than materialists to socially oriented entrepreneurship. Cross-country survey research on commercial entrepreneurialism finds that it correlates negatively with post-materialism, inferring that a reduced desire for economic achievement dampens profit-oriented business formation. This research also finds that the ratio of social to total entrepreneurialism across countries is positively correlated with a country's incidence of post-material values. Where post-materialism is relatively strong, so is social entrepreneurship. A country's per capita income positively correlates as well with the ratio of social to total entrepreneurialism. Wealth, post-materialism, and social entrepreneurship all move together.[11]

Poor countries, lacking a robust corporate sector, possess, out of material necessity, a large sector of small businesses, many of which are found in the "underground" economy. The first thing visitors to Cairo, Egypt will likely notice is that everywhere someone is trying to sell something. For many of the city's residents, small enterprises provide the only path to earning a living, and not very many of these can afford to pursue a social mission. Nonetheless, social enterprises exist in Egypt and other low-income countries. Remember, the incidence of early stage social entrepreneurs in poor countries average a non-trivial 1.3 percent in comparison to the 1.8 global average. Social entrepreneurship indeed occurs in low-income countries, and its incidence rises as development takes place along with growth in post-materialism.

One would think that Egypt, with its history of political oppression and military and oligarchical domination of key business sectors, would be the last place for substantial social entrepreneurialism. Nonetheless, we can find in this country fascinating examples of businesses working hard to solve social and environmental problems. Along the way we can also discover compatibility between a liberal post-materialism and a traditional Islamic philosophical orientation. Modern liberal Islamic scholars

---

[11]Lorraine Uhlaner and Roy Thurik, "Postmaterialism influencing total entrepreneurial activity across nations," *Journal of Evolutionary Economics* 17, no. 2 (2007).

argue that one can accept such post-materialist values as environmentalism and still be a Muslim.[12] Belief in the Koran, with its poetic descriptions of worldly being as God's creation, much like modern Christianity, can be reconciled with a modern commitment to personal freedom, economic justice, self-expression, and saving the environment. The theological justification for this view we leave to others and focus instead on its real world manifestation. If social entrepreneurship can flourish alongside Islam and under the political radar in Egypt, then there must be something to it.

***

Ibrahim Abouleish grew up in a mixed Arabic and Jewish Cairo neighborhood in the 1940s and 1950s, went to a Christian school, and became deeply attached to his Muslim faith at an early age. He attended university in Austria where he obtained a medical degree as well as training in research chemistry. After completing his studies, he carved out a successful career in pharmacological research in Austria, married an Austrian, and started a family. Dr. Abouleish has enjoyed and admired European culture throughout his life but remains a committed Muslim to this day, and, unlike many other Egyptians, expressed opposition to war with Israel in the 1960s.[13]

Although he returned to Egypt frequently to visit his family, Dr. Abouleish did not travel extensively in the country until 1975 when he took an eye-opening trip with an Austrian friend. He was shocked by the catastrophic degradation of agriculture in the Nile Valley and the physical decline of Cairo and its living conditions. Construction of the Aswan High Dam in his eyes was an unmitigated disaster in its halting of the age-old annual flooding of the Nile that covered fields with life-giving fertile mud. Farmers were forced to compensate for this loss of fertility by applying large amounts of fertilizer that in turn led to excessive soil salting and compression.

---

[12]Fazlun Khalid, "Islam and the Environment," in *Volume 5, Encyclopedia of Global Environmental Change*, ed. Peter Timmerman (Chichester: Wiley, 2002).
[13]Ibrahim Abouleish and Helmy Abouleish, "Garden in the Desert: Sekem Makes Comprehensive Sustainable Development a Reality " *Innovations* 3(2008); Ibrahim Abouleish, *Sekem: A Sustainable Community in the Egyptian Desert* (Edinburgh: Floris Books, 2005).

On his return to Austria, Dr. Abouleish investigated and pondered what had happened to Egypt and began to seek alternatives to the continued degradation of the rural landscape. He became especially interested in biodynamic agriculture, a type of organic farming developed by students of Rudolph Steiner's anthroposophy. This form of farming had been successfully used for decades in Europe, especially in Italy. After traveling and learning about biodynamic methods, Dr. Abouleish set aside his research career and, with his wife and children, moved back to Egypt in 1977 to establish an organic farm. The farm became the starting point for the Sekem initiative, whose name is taken from ancient Egyptian hieroglyphics for the life-giving vitality of the sun.

Sekem, headquartered at the original farm site north of Cairo, today includes five different companies that employ 1,800 people and produce and sell a variety of organic products including natural medicines, cereals, rice, vegetables, pasta, honey, jams, dates, spices, herbs, edible oils, herbal teas, juices, coffee, milk, eggs, beef, sheep, chicken, seeds, and organic cotton textiles and clothing. One company, ISIS, distributes more than 80 percent of the herbal teas sold in Egypt. Sekem currently operates five farms on reclaimed desert lands that provide almost a third of the company's organic raw materials and has created permanent "Fair Trade" ties with small farmers for the rest. Sekem's secret weapon in desert reclamation is compost, a product it both uses itself and sells to other farmers. Compost rich soil in deserts increases fertility and productivity, retains much more water than conventional farm soil (essential in an arid climate), and sequesters substantial amount of carbon in its accumulated organic matter.

While Sekem is a profitable venture, its goals and activities extend well beyond those of a conventional business. Sekem has successfully advanced its founding vision of creating ecologically sustainable oases in the desert where health-giving organic goods can be grown in a manner that helps to protect both the local and global environment. In and around these oases, Sekem seeks to create communities where individuals can not only improve their material condition, but also expand their educational and culture capabilities as well. In all its efforts, Sekem adheres to strict standards for the protection of human rights (including religious freedom), achievement of gender equity, and educational and cultural advancement as well as rigorous targets for environmental sustainability including carbon emissions reduction.

Through its Development Foundation, Sekem has established a school located on its headquarters farm serving 300 kindergarten, primary, and secondary students. The students come from a diversity of social backgrounds, including both Muslims and Christians, and the school emphasizes respect for all religions and contains both a mosque and chapel. In addition to following the Egyptian state curriculum, the school makes a special effort to provide courses in crafts, drama, dance, and music. Sekem has its own orchestra that performs in the local community and gives special support to the practice of Eurythmy, a dance form originating in Europe. The Foundation has also established a modern medical center nearby that serves 120 patients or more a day from employee families and the local community. The clinic offers a variety of outreach programs that address such issues as women's health, family planning, and sanitation. In addition to these efforts, the Foundation also offers vocational training and education in organic methods. The Sekem Academy located near Cairo undertakes applied research in agriculture and pharmaceuticals and helped to create the Heliopolis University that just recently opened and is offering degrees in pharmacy, engineering, and business. All students will take a set of core courses using a holistic approach to education focusing on culture, the environment, globalism, and the full development of personal abilities. In sum, Sekem in its short lifetime has created an impressive set of institutions with a visionary hope for realizing sustainable social and economic progress in the Egyptian countryside. How such a social invention occurred is a fascinating tale worth the telling.

Starting up something so unusual as an organic farm in an autocratic country dominated by the military and run by centralized bureaucracies proved to be a demanding and frustrating task. One day, bulldozers and soldiers arrived on the Sekem farm and started pulling down three-year old trees to clear the land. A local general had decided to turn the farm into a military area to take advantage of a water supply from wells dug for crops, and the intrusion was brought to a halt only because Dr. Abouleish was friends with President Sadat and could ask for his help.

One of the biggest challenges to Sekem arose from pesticide spraying on neighboring cotton fields spilling over onto the farm's medicinal herbs and other organic crops, threatening the company's certification as a biodynamic producer. Fearing a collapse in the cotton crop, the Egyptian government refused to curtail pesticide spraying. Sekem set out to prove on test plots that organic methods for controlling pests are just as functional and no more costly than conventional pesticide applications. After several years of testing, Sekem demonstrated the effectiveness of organic methods, and pesticide use was eventually halted on all of Egyptian cotton fields. As a reward for its efforts, Sekem successfully entered the organic cotton business.

Egyptian pesticide companies of course were unhappy about the loss of a lucrative market caused by Sekem and began a campaign to generate negative publicity against the company. Newspaper articles soon appeared suggesting that organic agriculture is unaffordable for poor countries like Egypt and that Sekem is a pawn of wealthy Europeans. The most damaging attack came with a widely circulated news report that the company's employees engaged in sun worship on the job, a practice seen as idolatrous and horrific to faithful Muslims. The news article grossly misrepresented a weekly employee assembly where all stand in a circle to emphasize the importance of each individual in the work of the whole and the equal dignity of everyone.

To combat attacks by prayer leaders in local mosques, Dr. Abouleish decided to invite all local Muslim community leaders, mayors, and sheiks to Sekem to show how the company's mission promotes important virtues of the Muslim faith. He used passages from the Koran to illustrate how organic agriculture meets the call for faithful Muslims to be "...responsible for the earth, plants and animals." To make his point, Dr. Abouleish quoted the following from the Koran along with other similar passages:

> The sun and the moon pursue their ordered course. The plants and the trees bow down in adoration. He [God]

---

[14]Abouleish and Abouleish, "Garden in the Desert: Sekem Makes Comprehensive Sustainable Development a Reality ".

raised the heaven on high and set the balance of all things, that you might not transgress it. Do not disrupt the equilibrium and keep the right measure and do not lose it.[14]

He continued in the meeting to explain exactly how biodynamic agricultural methods support the balance of nature more effectively than the kind of farming that makes heavy use of pesticides and fertilizers. The audience was impressed by the connection between organic agriculture and the call of the Koran for human stewardship of Earth and nature. Positive articles about Sekem soon appeared in the Egyptian media and public doubts about the company evaporated.

This brief summary of Sekem's overcoming of early tribulations offers only a partial and incomplete picture of its accomplishments. For a comprehensive account, I urge readers to take a look at Dr. Abouleish's book, *Sekem: A Sustainable Community in the Egyptian Desert*.[15]

The Sekem experience demonstrates a potential in Egyptian agricultural for expansion and employment growth while at the same time doing good turns for both rural communities and the environment. One of the biggest advantages Egypt and other North African countries possess for organic food production is their proximity to European markets. Demand in Europe for organics has been growing rapidly in recent years, and the ability of Egypt to provide crops in all seasons is a special competitive benefit. Because of their reduced demand for water relative to conventional crops, organics place less pressure on scarce water resources, and since organics don't require pesticides or synthetic fertilizers, a transition to organic cropping in and adjacent to the Nile Valley would substantially diminish the region's water pollution problems. The buildup and retention of carbon in organically cropped soils and the reduced dependence on fossil fuel based pesticides and fertilizers that comes from a transition to organics has the positive side-benefit of diminishing the impact of agriculture on climate change. Since organic methods are often more labor intensive than mechanized conventional agriculture, a shift in cropping to organics would in itself increase employment. Perhaps the biggest

---

[15]Ibrahim Abouleish, *Sekem: A Sustainable Community in the Egyptian Desert* (Edinburgh: Floris Books, 2005).

benefit of Sekem's approach is its practice of creating farms on desert lands through the addition of compost to the soil and the development of highly efficient irrigation systems using deep wells. In this way, Egyptian agricultural production is expanded without placing added pressure on scarce Nile Valley land and water resources. Sekem can't be accused of ignoring the Egyptian need for good food since almost 70 percent of its total sales occur in the domestic market. The lucrative export market essentially provides added financial heft to Sekem for investing in domestic agriculture to the benefit of Egypt as a whole. The point is simple: expansion of organic agriculture in Egypt and elsewhere can be good for both economic development and the environment, and in this endeavor Sekem offers an enticing model for solving a multitude of economic, social, and environmental problems in rural areas of the Middle East.

Ibrahim Abouleish is just one man who has successfully sought an intersection between the Muslim faith and European post-materialist values. In his life, he orients himself both to the tenants of Islam, and to self-expression, individual freedom, tolerance for human differences, and environmental protection. Islamic scholars have little trouble constructing an environmental ethics rooted in the Koran, but whether such ethics will matter much in the future remains an open question. The Sekem experience points at least to the potential for a sea change in Islamic environmental practice with Muslim social entrepreneurs, such as Ibrahim Abolish, leading the charge to a better environmental and economic future.

***

To backyard gardeners who love to muck around in real dirt, growing plants in water somehow seems otherworldly, but the science of doing so, known as hydroponics, is a well-established technology. Soil in natural conditions serves as a reservoir for water and plant nutrients, but plants don't actually require soil to survive. Plants in fact absorb nutrients through their roots as inorganic mineral ions dissolved in water. So long as plant roots have access to water containing essential minerals, plants can survive without soil. Since plant survival also requires access to oxygen through roots, roots cannot be completely and perpetually immersed in water unless it is adequately aerated or else the plants will drown. Plants can be grown hydroponically in solution using something as simple as water in a Mason jar, but more frequently growers use an inert medium in which to grow plants such as perlite, gravel, mineral wool, or coconut husk.

Hydroponic gardening has virtues that offer special advantages for growing plants in an arid climate like Egypt's. In soil-based farming, applying the right amount of water is a tricky business. Too much watering causes plants to die from a lack of oxygen, and too little leads to plant starvation. For hydroponic farming, plant roots can be continuously or frequently exposed to nutrient-laden water and the plants can absorb as much or as little as they want. Unused water can be drained away and recycled keeping water use to a bare minimum. The key challenge for the hydroponic approach is to get the balance of needed mineral in the water just right, including macronutrients such as nitrates, calcium, phosphate, and magnesium, and micronutrients such as iron, copper, zinc, boron, chlorine and nickel. In addition to an appropriate balance of nutrients, care must be taken to not let the water's pH get out of whack or salts to build up excessively. Any interruption in water flows can be catastrophic, and water must be stored in light-free tanks to prevent the formation of algae. A successful hydroponic system can achieve high levels of productivity with a modest water and nutrient input.[16]

The other central ingredient in plant growth is sunshine, something that Egyptian rooftops have in abundance year around. The country's low-income residents have long used rooftops to raise chickens and goats but not to grow crops. Looking out over Cairo's rooftops from a minaret or any other high vantage points, one sees mostly accumulated debris, satellite dishes, and virtually nothing green. The dream of social entrepreneur, Sherif Hosny, is to green up the city's rooftops by creating on them hundreds of hydroponic gardens in the city's poorest neighborhoods. Hosny appropriately named the business, Schaduf, after a simple traditional Egyptian farm tool from raising water to higher ground for crop irrigation, and why not to rooftops?

---

[16] Yusif Genc, Julie Hayes, and Yuri Shavrukov, "Hydroponics: A Standard Methodology for Plant Biological Researches," ResearchGate,
http://www.researchgate.net/publication/233927805_Hydroponics_-_A_Standard_Methodology_for_Plant_Biological_Researches?ev=pub_srch_pub.

Schaduf offers Cairo's low-income residents a simple but functional and efficient form of hydroponic farming. Construct on a family's rooftop three 20 square meter ponds made of brick sides about 10 centimeters high and place a waterproof liner on the inner surface, fill with water and cover with sheets of floating styrofoam to serve as a platform for plants, and install a circulating pump for oxygenating the water. Add a standard hydroponic nutrient mix and plant the seedlings. Come by and check the pH and electrolyte levels weekly, replenish nutrients as needed, and soon with the help of Egypt's sun and heat you will have a rooftop of green produce that can be sold for 300-500 Egyptian pounds a month, significantly increasing a Cairene's family income and creating a wonderful place for children to play that pulls them away from the dangers of the streets. Sherif's company, Schaduf Urban Micro Farms, will provide a poor family with a rooftop farm costing about 4,000 Egyptian pounds that can be financed with a microloan easily paid off in a year. Schaduf then helps maintain each farm, periodically checking the nutrient mix and controlling any pests organically, and also collects and sells the produce in a local Zamalek farmer's market for its clients.[17]

While visiting Cairo, my wife and I, along with our son and his boss, ate a celebratory dinner costing 1,000 Egyptian pounds at a fancy restaurant on the Nile called the Sequoia, a place where Cairenes go to be seen. This means roughly that a low-income rooftop garden costs about 4 Sequoia meal equivalents, an amount of money that doesn't mean much to us affluent westerners, but can make a huge difference to the lives of Cairo's urban farmers.

Leaving a successful career as the Middle East Regional Managing Director for mining Giant Rio Tinto Alcan, Sherif Hosny moved on to become a creator of rooftop gardens. Ask him why he gave up a lucrative career to take up urban farming, and he will tell you that he wants to help others, likes working with plants, and desires to earn enough income to live on. In these motivations, Hosny differs little from Ibrahim Abouleish, the founder of Sekem. While he grew up in a Muslim family, Hosni doesn't claim that his

---

[17]Megan Detrie, "'Schaduf' sets up rooftop urban farms for low-income families," *Egypt Independent*, March 16, 2012.

faith played any special role in his decision to found Schaduf, yet what he is doing satisfies Islamic premises much like Sekem does.

Hosny chose to do a business rather than a nongovernmental organization (NGO) so he wouldn't have to worry about raising money for operations, and he wanted the people he helps to have a vested interest themselves in sustaining the final product, the rooftop farm. If nothing else, Schaduf's clients will work hard to pay back the micro-loans they take out for their farms, and once they do, their take-home income jumps, encouraging them to keep their efforts up. NGOs are a part of the picture for rooftop farming and make a difference for Schaduf by helping to identify eligible clients and arranging micro-loans. The beauty of the whole venture is that it is self-funding and can be readily scaled up as the business grows.

Hosny continues to work on new ideas for rooftop farming, including an organic nutrient mix to replace the standard chemical variety. Schaduf's most important innovation to date has been the development of the simple brick-sided floor pond to replace the usual wooden racks hydroponic gardeners typically use to support plant trays, which turn out to be uneconomical in Cairo because wood is too expensive. In the past Hosny experimented with an aquaponic approach to micro farming using tilapia, but the fish couldn't survive Cairo's winter temperatures in the shallow tanks required by a rooftop location, and heaters proved to costly for his low-income clients. Schaduf also sells rooftop hydroponic gardens to more affluent customers who want to grow their own plants and create a green space for their family. Doing so augments Schaduf's sales and income and increases the scale and efficiency of its operation, allowing the venture to better serve its low-income farmers.

Sherif Hosny fits the classic definition of a social entrepreneur, someone engaged in business to solve social or environmental problems, not just to earn profit. Hosny and Schaduf help poor families increase their income, expand the supply of healthy greens for Cairenes, and create much needed green space in a city that has very little. In this effort, Schaduf engages in social invention—the search for new and innovative methods for solving social and environmental problems. Schaduf not only applies a time-tested technology in a new way, but also creates a new form of pesticide-free agriculture that functions without substantial fossil fuel inputs and requires very little water, a huge benefit in a desert environment. Schaduf, like any other entrepreneurial venture may or may not work out, and if it doesn't Hosny will move onto something else. Given the important functions Schaduf fulfills, I suspect that it will succeed and contribute to a better future for Egyptians.

***

Ahmed Zahran grew up in Cairo, received a bachelor's degree from the city's American University, and a masters from the University of London. While he never was exposed to renewable energy in his studies, he gained an interest in it early on, and wanted to make a career of it. Because of a lack of opportunities in Egypt, Zahran went work for Shell Oil Company and eventually landed in the company's carbon emissions trading department. Here it soon became clear to him that the only way to reduce emissions was to shift from fossil fuels to solar, and his work at Shell was not going to help much in achieving that goal.[18]

Zahran returned to Egypt and went to work for a solar energy company that unfortunately succumbed to the upheaval of the Arab Spring. This experience led Zahran to join with some friends in founding KarmSolar for the purpose of developing solar energy applications to serve the challenges of rural Egyptians who live in desert landscapes. KarmSolar quickly gained global attention for its work on high capacity off-grid solar water pumps that recover underground water from very deep wells for agricultural uses. The premise of KarmSolar is to offer Egyptians the opportunity to live in off-grid desert communities and have access to unexploited groundwater resources available on the edges of the Nile Valley and desert oases. The idea is to pull population away from an overcrowded Nile and take advantage of the desert's abundance of sun and soil much like Sekem has done.

The standard approach for Nile Valley irrigation agriculture is to mindlessly flood the fields periodically to supply water to plants. On reclaimed desert lands, groundwater is too scarce and flooding too wasteful. Movable sprinklers and drip irrigation

---

[18]Steven Viney, "KarmSolar Develops Renewable Energy Solution for 'Off Grid' Farmers," *Egypt Indepedent*, March 22, 2012.

systems offer a much more water efficient approach to growing crops. Sprinkler irrigation turns out not to be very effective for anything but low value fodder crops because of leaf salt-burn on broadleaf plants or problems with fungi forming because of water accumulation on leaf surfaces. Drip irrigation systems, with perforated plastic piping laid out in rows adjacent to vegetable or fruit plants, offer a highly efficient method of water and liquid fertilizer delivery to plant roots. In this sense, drip irrigation and hydroponic agriculture bear a similarity. Some drip irrigation farmers take advantage of a lucrative nearby European organic fruit and vegetable market by creating liquid organic fertilizer from animal manure onsite for delivery to plants through the irrigation system. One might think that a huge upfront investment requirement rules out all but big farms for drip irrigation, but already in desert landscapes big-farm hired workers learn the drip irrigation ropes and install inexpensive drip systems on their own nearby small plots.[19]

The big problem currently for agriculture on reclaimed Egyptian desert far away from an electrical grid is dependence on diesel powered generators that require difficult to deliver and expensive liquid fuels for their operation. The big advantage offered by the KarmSolar approach is an independent local source of electrical power that can run irrigation pumps and other kinds of equipment such as water purifiers and desalinators. The marriage of solar power and water efficient-irrigation makes feasible the creation of new communities in the desert wherever groundwater can be found. Not only does this opportunity allow KarmSolar to make money to sustain itself, but also opens up a chance for Egyptians to find a new ways of making a living without having to depend on an unreliable electrical grid or an incompetent central government. This is to the liking of social entrepreneurs such as KarmSolar's Ahmed Zahran and Schaduf's Sherif Hosny who both express exasperation with government incompetence. It's fascinating to see entrepreneurial efforts with both a social and an

---

[19]H.K. Soussa, "Effects of Drip Irrigation Water Amount on Crop Yield, Productivity and Efficiency of Water Use in Desert Regions in Egypt," *Nile Basin Water Science & Engineering Journal* 3(2010); Mona Mourshed, "Rethinking Irrigation Technology Adoption: Lessons from the Egyptian Desert," in *Working Paper Number 23, Program in Science, Technology, and Society* (Cambridge: MIT, 1995).

environmental mission, such as Sekem, Schaduf, and KarmSolar, gaining a foothold under the radar of government ineffectiveness and political upheaval, and in the context of a strongly traditional Muslim culture.

***

If it can stand the kind of political stresses experienced in Egypt, then social entrepreneurship should be able to flourish elsewhere in more settled and affluent environments. While our Egyptian entrepreneurs don't directly focus on creating economic democracy in the form of large-scale worker-owned businesses, they have advanced economic independence for the people they serve, an important prerequisite for economic equity and personal autonomy. Let's now top off our discussion of economic democracy with an American case of two socially minded entrepreneurs who explicitly set out to create an environmentally responsible, employee-owned business, New Belgium Brewing Company headquartered in Fort Collins, Colorado.[20]

The brewing industry in the past 25 years has gone no-where in terms of its total sales volume, but it's the production details that reveal a qualitative revolution within. For years, brewing has been dominated by a few huge industrial producers such Anheuser-Busch, Coors, and Miller, cranking out beers that all pretty much taste the same. To sample a variety of interesting beer in this era of big brewery dominance, an American had to take a vacation to Belgium or Germany. Since the 1980s, an innovative bunch of craft brewers have invaded the industry, bringing with them beers that actually taste like something. From 2007 to 2012, total U.S. beer production shrank from 214 million to about 210 million barrels while craft brewing increased from about 9 million barrels to 14 million. The American public clearly wants more diverse and better tasting beer offerings, and the craft beer industry is fulfilling their desires. By 2020, craft beer is projected to take over 20 percent of the total beer market.[21] Today, New Belgium Brewing, one of the leaders of the craft brewing revolution, is closing in on

---

[20]Christopher Asher, Elina Bidner, and Christopher Greene, "New Belgium Brewing Company: Brewing With a Conscience," (Denver: The Graduate School of Public Affairs, University of Colorado at Denver and Health Science Center, 2003).
[21]Demeter Group, "State of the Craft Beer Industry," (San Francisco: Demeter Group Investment Bank, 2013).

800,000 barrels in annual production, putting it in the number three slot for sales in craft brewing, and will soon open a new brewery in Asheville, North Carolina that will help solidify its front row seat in the industry.[22]

New Belgium got its start in the brewing business after an inspirational mountain biking trip to Europe in 1986 by one of its founders, Jeff Lebesch, an electrical engineer. On this trip he gained a special affection for Belgian style ales, and on his return to Fort Collins, Colorado, Jeff set about learning the art of Belgian-inspired brewing in his home. His ales soon became popular with friends, and he and his wife, Kim Jordan, started brewing commercially for the local market in 1991. Kim had a special talent for marketing and distribution, and sales grew rapidly led by Fat Tire Amber Ale named for Jeff's European biking adventure. A fat tire mountain bike became the defining symbol for the new brewery, and today each employee who stays at least a year gets a "Fat Tire" cruiser town bike for getting around Fort Collins. In 1995 after outgrowing operations in a former railroad depot, New Belgian moved into a new, environmentally friendly state of the art brewing facility. This new brewery concretely manifested the company's mission statement, "to operate a profitable company which is socially, ethically, and environmentally responsible, that produces high quality beer true to the Belgian styles."[23] By this time, the founders had begun transferring shares in the company to its workers through an Employee Stock Ownership Plan (ESOP). In 1998, an environmental audit revealed that the company's single largest source of CO_2 emissions came, not from fermentation as many thought, but from electricity consumption. The company founders proposed to shift completely to wind power in order to reduce carbon emissions, and put the proposal up to a vote by employee-owners who approved it despite increased costs and reductions in profits that would follow.

The simplest, most financially advantageous path to employee ownership in this country is through the establishment of an ESOP. For founders of businesses like New Belgium who want their

---

[22]New Belgium Brewing, "Rankings," New Belgium Brewing, http://www.newbelgium.com/brewery/company/craft-beer-rankings-and-financials.aspx.
[23]Asher, Bidner, and Greene, "New Belgium Brewing Company: Brewing With a Conscience."

workers to gain an ownership stake, an ESOP greases the skids to such a goal by offering significant tax benefits. Businesses can make tax-deductible annual contributions to an ESOP trust for the purchase of stock shares from founders to be held on behalf of employees until they retire or leave the company. Alternatively, an ESOP trust can borrow funds to buy shares for participants with the business making tax deductible annual contributions to pay back the loan not to exceed 25 percent of plan participant annual total payroll.[24] New Belgium recently announced that its ESOP trust now owns 100 percent of the shares, meaning that the company is fully worker-owned.[25] By way of an ESOP, founders can at the same time retain a management role in the company, cash out their ownership share, and provide a retirement benefit to employees. An ESOP creates an opportunity for economic democracy, such as employees voting on whether to use only carbon-free energy despite its greater cost, but it doesn't require it. The only absolute requirement is that worker-owners have a say in whether their company is sold to a third party. An ESOP can in theory be structured in its bylaws along the lines of a Mondragon cooperative so that employees choose members of a company's governing board.

The point of the New Belgium case is to substantiate that employee ownership and the greater economic equity that goes with it is feasible in this country. In the U.S. today some 7,000 ESOPs cover nearly 14,000,000 workers.[26] For the continued expansion of this kind of economic democracy, and a turn to more participatory forms akin to Mondragon, the need is for more socially minded entrepreneurs who want to make money but also have a vision to do some good for society along the way. Globally, post-materialists favor "having more say" and "doing something worthwhile" in their working lives over the pure "make as much money as you can" approach to business. For this reason alone,

---

[24]National Center for Employee Ownership, "How an Employee Stock Ownership Plan (ESOP) Works," National Center for Employee Ownership, http://www.nceo.org/articles/esop-employee-stock-ownership-plan.
[25]New Belgium Blog, "We are 100% Employee Owned," New Belgium Brewing, http://www.newbelgium.com/community/Blog/13-01-16/We-are-100-Employee-Owned.aspx.
[26]National Center for Employee Ownership, "How an Employee Stock Ownership Plan (ESOP) Works".

more economic democracy may be on the horizon, a hopeful prospect for pragmatic liberals who seek a more participatory society, greater material equity, and more business concern with the social problems of the day.

13 Our Post-Material Future

I am one of those rare beasts, a member of the Silent Generation who considers himself a post-materialist. My future probably has a shorter time horizon than yours, so you are more likely than me to actually experience manifestations of the post-material turn. Right now, political and economic reality doesn't look very post-materialist, but we can take heart in a different future. If you are of a liberal or progressive inclination, you will be pleased, but if you have conservative leanings, you may not be entirely happy. I suspect we can all agree that more expansive freedom of expression, personal autonomy, a more humane society, and wider public influence on political issues—key post-material values—will be seen as good things whatever our political leanings. I also suspect that conservatives will not be too keen on giving higher priority to such values as these than to the classic materialist goals such as economic expansion and stability, maintaining public order, and defending the country. The global political divide between progressive post-materialists and conservative materialists unfortunately will likely remain for some time.

While economic materialism continues to rule the day for most of us, this book attests to inklings of a slowly unfolding and different post-material future. This new vision of life pushes economic concerns down the priority scale, especially for younger generations, and moves social priorities up. Post-materialists especially support expressive freedom for all and a substantive tolerance for social diversity. Many also emphasize in their personal philosophy a commitment to economic equity, protection of the earth's natural treasures, and spiritual individuality. Post-materialists in their economic lives deemphasize the acquisition of material goods in favor of qualitative experiences. Symptomatic of this movement is the turning away by youthful Millennials from the suburbs and towards more densely packed and culturally rich urban centers as places to live and work. These same Millennials also give a higher priority to creative and expressive experiences in the work place than to earning a substantially greater income. Work at its best gives us a platform for autonomous creative expression, and at its worse can be meaningless and boring and serve only the need to earn an income. When sufficiently remunerative, a part time job can sidestep the problem of unsatisfying work and permit one to seek artistic and other kinds of creative expression outside the confines of formal employment. For this reason, a future post-material society will likely feature fewer working hours and more leisure for many of its members. Not all work can be creatively fulfilling, but some is essential for material sustenance. A strengthened desire for creative self-expression for many will require fulfillment outside the workplace, and for this reason I suspect paid work will diminish in importance as we move to a post-material future.

Such a future could also well do the natural global environment a big favor. An entropic experience is one that causes high volumes of energy and materials to move from concentrated and useful forms to those that are highly dispersed, useless, and frequently harmful to humanity and nature. Post-materialists purposefully and inadvertently engage in less entropic experiences than their materialist elders, giving the reversal of climatic warming a fighting chance. The ultimate magnitude of climate change comes down to a race for the global heart and mind between an entropy causing but powerful fossil fuel industry and the rising influence of post-materialists worried about the ultimate fate of the planet. In a post-material experience economy, materially benign acts of consumption rise in prominence. Instead of focusing predominantly on a private accumulation of material possessions, human attention will be drawn more to materially efficient shared experiences, such as strolling through a public park, enjoying a street corner musician, playing a pickup game of frisbee, or hiking a mountain trail with beautiful wildflowers and great views. Compact downtown urban living by its nature offers greater shared experience and claims less material and energy resources than its spatially expansive suburban counterpart to the benefit of the global environment.

Little that's new in the world is without its disruptions and challenges. The essential macro problem of a post-material economy is a serious dampening of the consumer spending inclination, a big deal in an economy where consumption adds up to 65-70 percent of total GDP. Spending decline by consumers in the private sector can always be offset by balancing increases in the public sector, to the consternation of the "red-state" side of the political divide in this country. Oddly, even politically liberal Europeans don't get the wisdom of shifting the spending balance in a public direction whenever the private sector isn't up to the task. For their absence of this "Keynesian" wisdom, Europe continues to suffer extraordinary unemployment rates. Ironically, Americans have taken Keynesian wisdom to heart (despite intense opposition) and avoided a deeper Great Recession as a consequence. This experience offers a lesson in how to avoid economic decline from a dampening of growth post-material consumption by undertaking an offsetting expansion of government expenditures. European economic experience does offer a positive alternative for avoiding rising unemployment from reduced consumer spending growth, and that is for everyone to simply work fewer hours as their productivity and hourly wage rates grow over time. While Europeans don't do so well with Keynesian economics, the do understand that wage gains from rising productivity can be used to expand leisure by shortening working hours instead of for increasing consumer spending.

History teaches us that the presence of excessive wealth and income inequality creates more of the same, especially under the reign of a free-market capitalism, and this can upset the post-materialist apple cart by consigning a big chunk of the population to an insufficient living standard. A simple answer to this problem is to make everyone a capitalist by way of employee ownership and economic democracy. Given the separation of capital ownership and work in our modern corporate world, economic democracy seems like a pipe dream, but it may blend nicely with the new trend to social entrepreneurship. Post-materialist entrepreneurs want to earn a decent income from their efforts at, say, starting new businesses, but they often want to do something for society, and especially for their own employees. One way for a social entrepreneur to "cash out" of a business to the benefit of those employees who helped get it up and running in the first place is to sell it to them through an Employee Stock Ownership Plan. In this way, the motivational barrier to forming worker-owned businesses and creating economic democracy dissolves in a post-material world where social and economic ends come into balance.

Again, all the future possibilities described in this book sound like inspiring music to a liberal's social and political ears, but we must be fully aware that these depend on the continuation of the current post-material trend in humanity's philosophical outlook. Plenty can go wrong along the way. Powerful vested economic and political interests wedded to current arrangements may win out in the political arena. The tendency to post-material values may well be limited by an inherent human conservatism giving continued sustenance to economic materialism and a political emphasis on social stability. I am no more skilled at predicting the future than anyone else. I merely want to point to the growing evidence for a rising human interest in post-materialism and to its possibilities for our economic future.

Bibliography

Abouleish, Ibrahim. *Sekem: A Sustainable Community in the Egyptian Desert*. Edinburgh: Floris Books, 2005.

Abouleish, Ibrahim, and Helmy Abouleish. "Garden in the Desert: Sekem Makes Comprehensive Sustainable Development a Reality ". *Innovations* 3 (2008): 21-48.

Abramson, Paul R., and Ronald F. Inglehart. *Value Change in Global Perspective*. Ann Arbor: University of Michigan Press, 1995.

Ahern, Lee. "The Role of Media System Development in the Emergence of Postmaterialist Values and Environmental Concern: A Cross-National Analysis." *Social Science Quarterly* 93, no. 2 (2012): 538-57.

Alesina, Alberto, Edward Glaeser, and Bruce Sacerdote. "Work and Leisure in the United States and Europe: Why So Different?". Chap. 1 In *NBER Macroeconomics Annual 2005*, edited by Mark Gertler and Kenneth Rogoff. Cambridge: MIT Press, 2005.

Alper, Neil O., and Gregory H. Wassall. "Artists' Careers and Their Labor Markets." Chap. 23 In *Handbook of the Economics of Art and Culture*, edited by Victor A. Ginsburgh and David Throsby. Amsterdam: North-Holland, 2006.

Arando, Saioa, Fred Freundlich, Monica Gago, Derek C. Jones, and Takao Kato. "Assessing Mondragon: Stability & Managed Change in the Face of Globalization." Ann Arbor: The William Davidson Institute, 2010.

Asghar, Rob. "What Millennials Want in the Workplace (and Why You Should Start Giving It to Them)." Forbes, http://www.forbes.com/sites/robasghar/2014/01/13/what-millennials-want-in-the-workplace-and-why-you-should-start-giving-it-to-them/.

Asher, Christopher, Elina Bidner, and Christopher Greene. "New Belgium Brewing Company: Brewing with a Conscience." Denver: The Graduate School of Public Affairs, University of Colorado at Denver and Health Science Center, 2003.

Ateca-Amestoy, Victoria M., and Juan Prieto-Rodriguez. "Forecasting Accuracy of Behavioral Models for Participation in the Arts." In *ACEI Working Paper Series*. Oviedo, Spain: Association for Cultural Economics, 2011.

Barro, Josh. "Voters Will Decide Minimum Wages in Four States Tuesday." *New York Times*, November 3 2014.

Baumol, W. J., and W. G. Bowen. "On the Performing Arts: The Anatomy of Their Economic Problems." *American Economic Review* 55, no. 1/2 (1965): 495-502.

Beckers, Tilo, Pascal Siegers, and Anabel Kuntz. "Congruence and Performance of Value Concepts in Social Research." *Survey Research Methods* 6 (2012): 13-24.

Birch, Eugenie L. "Who Lives Downtown?". Washington D.C.: Brookings Institution, 2005.

Booth, Douglas E. *The Coming Good Boom: Creating Prosperity for All and Saving the Environment through Compact Living*. Charleston: Create Space, 2010.

———. *Hooked on Growth: Economic Addictions and the Environment*. Lanham: Rowman & Littlefield, 2004.

Botvar, Pal Ketil. "Alternative Religion – a New Political Cleavage?: An Analysis of Norwegian Survey Data on New Forms of Spirituality." *Politics and Religion* 2 (2009): 378-94.

Brack, Jessica. "Maximizing Millennials in the Workplace." Chapel Hill UNC Kenan-Flagler Business School, 2014.

Center for Women and Business. "Millennials in the Workplace." Waltham, MA: Center for Women and Business, Bentley University, 2012.

Center, Pew Research. "Millenials: Confident, Connected, Open to Change." 2010.

———. "Millennials in Adulthood: Detached from Institutions, Networked with Friends." 2014.

Chang, Chum-chih, and Te-Sheng Chen. "Idealism Versus Reality: Empirical Test of Postmaterialism in China and Taiwan." *Issues and Studies* 49, no. 2 (June 2013): 63-102.

Daly, Herman, E. *Steady-State Economics*. Edited by 2nd. Washington D.C.: Island Press, 1991.

Detrie, Megan. "'Schaduf' Sets up Rooftop Urban Farms for Low-Income Families." *Egypt Independent*, March 16, 2012.

Dewan, Shaila. "How Obamacare Could Unlock Job Opportunities." *New York Times*, February 14, 2014.
Diener, Ed, and Robert Biswas-Diener. "Will Money Increase Subjective Well-Being?: A Literature Review and Guide to Needed Research." *Social Indicators Research* 37 (2009): 119-54.
Diener, Ed, Richard E. Lucas, and Christie Napa Scollon. "Beyond the Hedonic Treadmill: Revising the Adaptation Theory of Well-Being." *Social Indicators Research* 37 (2009): 103-18.
Diener, Ed, and Martin Seligman. "Beyond Money: Toward an Economy of Well-Being." *Social Indicators Research Series* 37 (2009): 201-65.
Dutzik, Tony, Jeff Inglis, and Phineas Baxandall. "Milleniansl in Motion: Changing Travel Habits of Young Americans and the Implications for Public Policy." Boston: U.S. PIRG Education Fund, 2014.
Edwards, Douglas. *I'm Feeling Lucky: The Confessions of Google Employee Number 59*. New York: Houghton Mifflin, 2011.
Errasti, Anjel. "Mondragon's Chinese Subsidiaries: Coopitalist Multinationals in Practice." *Economic and Industrial Democracy* Forthcoming (published online eid.sagepub.com) (2013).
Errasti, Anjel, Inaki Heras, Baleren Bakaikoa, and Pilar Elgoibar. "The Internationalisation of Cooperatives: The Case of the Mondragon Cooperative Corporation." *Annals of Public and Cooperative Economics* 74, no. 4 (2003): 553-84.
Feuer, Alan. "On the Move, in a Thriving Tech Sector." *New York Times* November 19, 2011.
Florida, Richard. *The Rise of the Creative Class: And How It's Transforming Work, Leisure, Community and Everyday Life*. New York: Basic Books, 2002.
Franzen, A., and R. Meyer. "Environmental Attitudes in Cross-National Perspective: A Multilevel Analysis of the ISSP 1993 and 2000." *European Sociological Review* 26, no. 2 (2009): 219-34.
Franzen, Axel, and Dominikus Vogl. "Acquiescence and the Willingness to Pay for Environmental Protection: A

Comparison of the ISSP, WVS, and EVS." *Social Science Quarterly* 94, no. 3 (2013): 637-59.
Garhammer, Manfred. "Pace and Enjoyment of Life." *Journal of Happiness Studies* 3 (2002): 217-56.
Gelissen, John. "Explaining Popular Support for Environmental Protection: A Multilevel Analysis of 50 Nations." *Environment and Behavior* 39, no. 3 (2007): 392-415.
Genc, Yusif, Julie Hayes, and Yuri Shavrukov. "Hydroponics: A Standard Methodology for Plant Biological Researches." ResearchGate, http://www.researchgate.net/publication/233927805_Hydroponics_-_A_Standard_Methodology_for_Plant_Biological_Researches?ev=pub_srch_pub.
Gerhards, Jurgen, and Holger Lengfeld. "Support for European Union Environmental Policy by Citizens of Eu-Member and Accession States." *Comparative Sociology* 7 (2008): 1-27.
Gilbert, Daniel. *Stumbling on Happiness*. New York: Knopf, 2006.
Givens, J. E., and A. K. Jorgenson. "The Effects of Affluence, Economic Development, and Environmental Degradation on Environmental Concern: A Multilevel Analysis." *Organization & Environment* 24, no. 1 (2011): 74-91.
Group, Demeter. "State of the Craft Beer Industry." San Francisco: Demeter Group Investment Bank, 2013.
Gruber, Jonathan, and Brigitte C. Madrian. "Health Insurance, Labor Supply, and Job Mobility: A Critical Review of the Literature." In *Working Paper 8817*. Cambridge: National Bureau of Economic Research, 2002.
Hagevi, Magnus. "Beyond Church and State: Private Religiosity and Post-Materialist Political Opinion among Individuals in Sweden." *Journal of Church and State* 54 (2012): 499-525.
Haidt, Jonathan. *The Righteous Mind: Why Good People Are Divided by Politics and Religion*. New York: Random House, 2012.
Hayden, A. "Work-Time Reduction and the Dutch Economic Miracle." Toronto: 32 Hours: Action for Full Employment, 1999.

Heidegger, Martin. *Being and Time*. Translated by John Macquarrie and Edward Robinson. Oxford: Blackwell, 1962.
———. "Building Dwelling Thinking." In *Martin Heidegger: Basic Writings*, edited by David Farrell Krell. 343-64. San Francisco: Harper, 1992.
———. "The Origin of the Work of Art." In *Martin Heidegger: Basic Writings*, edited by David Farrell Krell. 139-212. San Francisco: Harper, 1992.
———. "The Question Concerning Technology." In *Martin Heidegger: Basic Writings*, edited by David Farrell Krell. 307-42. San Francisco: Harper, 1992.
———. *What Is Called Thinking?* Translated by J. Glenn Gray. New York: Harper, 1976.
Hoogendoorn, Brigitte, and Chantal Hartog. "Prevalence and Determinants of Social Entrepreneurshp at the Macro-Level." In *EIM Research Reports*. Zoetermeer: Panteia/EIM, 2011.
Houtman, Dick, and Stef Aupers. "The Spiritual Turn and the Decline of Tradition: The Spread of Post-Christian Spirituality in 14 Western Countries, 1981–2000." *Journal for the Scientific Study of Religion* 46 (2007): 305-20.
Inglehart, Ronald F. "Changing Values among Western Publics from 1970 to 2006." *West European Politics* 31, no. 1-2 (2008): 130-46.
———. "Public Support for Environmental Protection: Objective Problems and Subjective Values in 43 Societies." *Political Science and Politics* 28 (1995): 57-72.
———. "The Worldviews of Islamic Publics in Global Perspective." Chap. 2 In *Values and Perceptions of the Islamic and Middle Eastern Publics*, edited by Mansoor Moaddel. 25-46. New York: Palgrave, 2007.
Inglehart, Ronald F., and Paul R. Abramson. "Economic Security and Value Change." *American Political Science Review* 88 (1994): 336-54.
Inglehart, Ronald F., and Wayne E. Baker. "Modernization, Cultural Change, and the Persistence of Traditional Values." *American Sociological Review* 65 (2000): 19-51.

Jacobs, Jane. *The Death and Life of Great American Cities.* New York: Vintage, 1961.

Kenny, Judith T., and Jeffrey Zimmerman. "Constructing the 'Genuine American City': Neo-Traditionalism, New Urbanism and Neo-Liberalism in the Remaking of Downtown Milwaukee." *Cultural Geographies* 11 (2003): 74-98.

Kenworthy, J.R. "Transport Energy Use and Greenhouse Gases in Urban Passenger Transport Systems: A Study of 84 Global Cities." Murdoch, Western Australia: Murdoch University, 2003.

Khalid, Fazlun. "Islam and the Environment." In *Volume 5, Encyclopedia of Global Environmental Change*, edited by Peter Timmerman. 332-39. Chichester: Wiley, 2002.

Krugman, Paul. *End This Depression Now!* New York: W.W. Norton, 2012.

———. *The Return of Depression Economics and the Crisis of 2008.* New York: W.W. Norton, 2009.

Kuhn, Randall. "On the Role of Human Development in the Arab Spring." Boulder: Institute of Science, University of Colorado, 2011.

Kvaloy, Berit, Henning Finseraas, and Ola Listhaug. "The Publics' Concern for Global Warming: A Cross-National Study of 47 Countries." *Journal of Peace Research* 49 (2012): 11-22.

Lansing, Kevin J. "Gauging the Impact of the Great Recession." *FRBSF Economic Letter*, no. 2011-21 (July 11, 2011).

Liu, Xinsheng, Arnold Vedlitz, and Liu Shi. "Examing the Determinants of Public Environmental Concern, Evidence from National Public Surveys." *Environmental Science and Policty* 39 (2014): 77-94.

Lloyd, Richard. *Neo-Bohemia: Art and Commerce in the Postindustrial City.* New York: Routledge, 2006.

———. "Neo-Bohemia: Art and Neighborhood Redevelopment in Chicago." *Journal of Urban Affairs* 24 (2002): 517-32.

Lowrey, Annie, and Jonathan Weisman. "Health Care Law Projected to Cut the Labor Force." *New York Times*, February 4, 2014.

Markusen, A., and A. Gadwa. "Arts and Culture in Urban or Regional Planning: A Review and Research Agenda." *Journal of Planning Education and Research* 29, no. 3 (2010): 379-91.

Markusen, Ann, and Greg Schrock. "The Artistic Dividend: Urban Artistic Specialisation and Economic Development Implications." *Urban Studies* 43, no. 10 (2006): 1661-86.

Mourshed, Mona. "Rethinking Irrigation Technology Adoption: Lessons from the Egyptian Desert." In *Working Paper Number 23, Program in Science, Technology, and Society*. Cambridge: MIT, 1995.

Nagel, Thomas. *Mind and Cosmos: Why the Materialist Neo-Darwinian Conception of Nature Is Almost Certainly False*. Oxford: Oxford University Press, 2012.

National Center for Employee Ownership. "How an Employee Stock Ownership Plan (ESOP) Works." National Center for Employee Ownership, http://www.nceo.org/articles/esop-employee-stock-ownership-plan.

National Endowment for The Arts. "How a Nation Engages with Art: Highlights from the 2012 Survey of Public Participation in the Arts." Washington D.C.: National Endowment for the Arts, 2014.

Nawrotzki, Raphael. "The Politics of Environmental Concern: A Cross-National Analysis." *Organization & Environment* 25 (2012): 286-307.

New Belgium Blog. "We Are 100% Employee Owned." New Belgium Brewing, http://www.newbelgium.com/community/Blog/13-01-16/We-are-100-Employee-Owned.aspx.

New Belgium Brewing. "Rankings." New Belgium Brewing, http://www.newbelgium.com/brewery/company/craft-beer-rankings-and-financials.aspx.

Newman, Peter, and Jeffrey R. Kenworthy. *Sustainability and Cities: Overcoming Automobile Dependency*. Washington D.C.: Island Press, 1999.

Nickerson, Carol, Norbert Schwartz, Ed Diener, and Daniel Kahneman. "Zeroing in on the Dark Side of the American Dream: A Closer Look at the Negative Consequences of the Goal for Financial Success." *Psychological Science* 14 (2003): 531-36.

Nickerson, Carol, Norbert Schwarz, and Ed Diener. "Financial Aspirations, Financial Success, and Overall Life Satisfaction: Who? And How?". *Journal of Happiness Studies* 8, no. 4 (2007): 467-515.

Nietzsche, Friedrich. "Beyond Good and Evil: Prelude to a Philosophy of the Future." In *Basic Writings of Nietzsche*, edited by Walter Kaufmann. 179-436. New York: Random House, 2000.

———. "The Birth of Tragedy: Out of the Spirit of Music." In *Basic Writings of Nietzsche*, edited by Walter Kaufmann. 15-144. New York: Random House, 2000.

———. *The Dawn of Day*. Translated by J. M. Kennedy. London: Dover, 2007.

———. *The Gay Science*. Translated by Josefine Nauckhoff and Adrian Del Caro. Edited by Bernard Williams. Cambridge: Cambridge University Press, 2001.

———. *Human, All-Too-Human*. Translated by Helen Zimmern and Paul V. Cohn. Lawrence: Digireads.com, 2009.

———. *Thus Spoke Zarathustra: A Book for None and All*. Translated by Walter Kaufmann. New York: Penguin Books, 1978.

———. *Will to Power*. Translated by Anthony M. Ludovici. New York2006.

Okulicz-Kozaryn, Adam. "Europeans Work to Live and Americans Live to Work (Who Is Happy to Work More: Americans or Europeans)." *Journal of Happiness Studies* 12 (2011): 225-43.

Olson, Mancur. *The Logic of Collective Action: Public Goods and the Theory of Groups*. Cambridge: Harvard University Press, 1965.

Perkins, Harold A. "Green Spaces of Self-Interest within Shared Urban Governance." *Geography Compass* 4 (2010): 255-58.

Pew Research Center. "Millennials in Adulthood: Detached from Institutions, Networked with Friends." 2014.

Piketty, Thomas. *Capital in the Twenty-First Century*. Cambridge: Harvard University Press, 2014.

Polzin, Steven E., Xuehao Chu, and Jodi Godrey. "The Impact of Millennials' Travel Behavior on Future Personal Vehicle Travel." *Energy Strategy Reviews* http.//dx.doi.org/10.1016/j.esr.2014.10.003 (2014).
Reynolds, Jeremy. "You Can't Always Get the Hours You Want: Mismatches between Actual and Preferred Work Hours in the U.S." *Social Forces* 81, no. 4 (2003): 1171-99.
Rorty, Richard. *Contingency, Irony, and Solidarity*. Cambridge: Cambridge University Press, 1989.
———. *Philosophy and Social Hope*. New York: Penquin, 1999.
———. *Philosophy and the Mirror of Nature*. Princeton: Princeton University Press, 1979.
Rosenthal, Elisabeth. "The End of Car Culture." *New York Times*, June 29, 2013.
Rusli, Evelyn M. "Zynga's Tough Culture Risks a Talent Drain." *New York Times*, November 11, 2011.
Sahlins, Marshall. *Stone Age Economics*. London: Tavistock, 1974.
Sartre, Jean-Paul. *Being and Nothingness*. New York: Washington Square Press, 1992.
———. *Nausea*. New York: New Directions, 2007.
Schwartz, Shalom H. "Are There Universal Aspects in the Structure and Contents of Human Values?". *Journal of Social Issues* 50, no. 4 (1994): 19-45.
Shiller, Robert J. *Irrational Exuberance*. Second ed. Princeton: Princeton University Press, 2005.
———. *The Subprime Solution: How Today's Global Financial Crisis Happened and What to Do About It*. Princeton: Princeton University Press, 2008.
Sirgy, M. Joseph, and Jiyun Wu. "The Pleasant Life, the Engaged Life, and the Meaningful Life: What About the Balanced Life?". *Journal of Happiness Studies* 10, no. 2 (2007): 183-96.
Sousa-Poza, Alfonso, and Adres A. Sousa-Poza. "Well-Being at Work: A Cross-National Analysis of the Level and Determinants of Job Satisfaction." *Journal of Socio-Economics* 29 (2000): 517-38.
Soussa, H.K. "Effects of Drip Irrigation Water Amount on Crop Yield, Productivity and Efficiency of Water Use in Desert

Regions in Egypt." *Nile Basin Water Science & Engineering Journal* 3 (2010): 96-109.

Stiglitz, Joseph E. *Freefall: America, Free Markets, and the Sinking of the World Economy.* New York: W.W. Norton, 2010.

Strom, E. "Artist Garret as Growth Machine? Local Policy and Artist Housing in U.S. Cities." *Journal of Planning Education and Research* 29, no. 3 (2010): 367-78.

Thomas, Henk, and Chris Logan. *Mondragon: An Economic Analysis.* London: Allen and Unwin, 1982.

Tjernstrom, E., and T. Tietenberg. "Do Differences in Attitudes Explain Differences in National Climate Change Policies?". *Ecological Economics* 65 (2012): 315-24.

Tolan, Tom. *Riverwest: A Community History.* Milwaukee: Past Press, 2003.

Twenge, Jean M., W. Keith Campbell, and Elise C. Freeman. "Generational Differences in Young Adults' Life Goals, Concern for Others, and Civic Orientation, 1966-2009." *Journal of Personality and Social Psychology* 102, no. 5 (2012): 1045-62.

Twitchell, James B. *Lead Us into Temptation: The Triumph of the American Dream.* New York: Columbia University Press, 1999.

U.S. Bureau of Labor Statistics. "Consumer Spending and U.S. Employment from the 2007-2009 Recession through 2022." In, *Monthly Labor Review* (2014). Published electronically October 11, 2014. http://www.bls.gov/opub/mlr/2014/article/consumer-spending-and-us-employment-from-the-recession-through-2022.htm.

U.S. Council of Economic Advisors. "Economic Report of the President, 2014." Washington D.C.: U.S. Government Printing Office, 2014.

U.S. Energy Information Administration. "Annual Energy Review 2011." U.S. Energy Information Administration, www.eia.gov/totalenergy/data/annual/pdf/sec2.pdf.

Uhlaner, Lorraine, and Roy Thurik. "Postmaterialism Influencing Total Entrepreneurial Activity across Nations." *Journal of Evolutionary Economics* 17, no. 2 (2007): 161-85.

Viney, Steven. "Karmsolar Develops Renewable Energy Solution for 'Off Grid' Farmers." *Egypt Indepedent*, March 22, 2012.
Visser, Jelle. "The First Part-Time Economy in the World: A Model to Be Followed?". *Journal of European Social Policy* 12, no. 1 (2002): 23-42.
Walsh, Bryan. "The Surprisingly Large Energy Footprint of the Digital Economy " Time Magazine, http://science.time.com/2013/08/14/power-drain-the-digital-cloud-is-using-more-energy-than-you-think/.
Wei, Max, Shana Patadia, and Daniel M. Kammen. "Putting Renewables and Energy Efficiency to Work: How Many Jobs Can the Clean Energy Industry Generate in the U.S.?". *Energy Policy* 38 (2010): 919-31.
Welzel, Christian, and Ronald F. Inglehart. "The Role of Ordinary People in Democratization." *Journal of Democracy* 19 (2008): 126-40.
Young, Julian. *Friedrich Nietzsche: A Philosophical Biography*. Cambridge: Cambridge University Press, 2010.
———. *Heidegger's Later Philosophy*. Cambridge: Cambridge University Press, 2002.
Zahran, Sammy, Eunyi Kim, Xi Chen, and Mark Lubell. "Ecological Development and Global Climate Change: A Cross-National Study of Kyoto Protocol Ratification." *Society & Natural Resources* 20, no. 1 (2007): 37-55.
Zandi, Mark, and Alan S. Blinder. "How the Great Recession Was Brought to an End." West Chester, PA: Moody's Analytics, 2010.
Zimmerman, J. "From Brew Town to Cool Town: Neoliberalism and the Creative City Development Strategy in Milwaukee." *Cities* 25, no. 4 (2008): 230-42

Index

A

Abouleish, Ibrahim, 150, 152-155, 157
acid rain, 68
advertising, 6, 26-27
Aeropress espresso maker, 115, 124-125
Alchemist Theater, Milwaukee, Wisconsin, 31
Amazon, 20-22, 129
American University in Cairo, 158
anguish, 43, 47, 49
Anheuser-Busche, 161
anxiety, 1, 5, 25, 104-105, 107, 113
Apollo, 90-92, 97
Apple, 108
Arab oil embargo, 67
Arab Spring, 120, 159
Arizmendi, Don Jose Maria, 144-145, 147
arts, 31, 36-40, 42-49, 55-57, 84-88, 90, 118
Aswan Dam, 150
Athens, Greece, 91
Austria, 150
authentic vs. inauthentic life, 45, 47, 49, 104-106, 109-112, 119

B

Baby Boomers, 15-17
bad faith, 44, 47, 49
Bayview, Milwaukee, Wisconsin, 31-32, 48
Being/being, 1-3, 11-12, 42-49, 89-129, 149
Being and Nothingness, 43-46
Being and Time, 102
Belgium, 161-163
Beyond Good and Evil, 96
Birch, Eugenie, 34

Birth of Tragedy, 48, 90, 92
biodynamic agriculture, 150, 153
bohemia, 33, 38, 40, 42, 46, 48
branding, 26-28
Breitling watches, 26-27
brewing industry, 161
Brin, Sergey, 5, 147
Brookings Institution, 34

C

Caha Laboral, 142
Cairo, Egypt, 150, 152, 158
cap and trade, 23, 66, 68-71
Capital in the Twenty-First Century, 140
carbon dioxide emissions (CO_2), 58, 61-63, 67, 69-72, 79, 154, 162-163
carbon tax, 71
care for being, 102, 104-105, 110
Cass, Helen Langdon, 24
Catholic, 102, 112, 144
central city, 29-30, 35-36, 38-39, 41, 49, 57, 79, 82
charity, 93-94
Cheerios, 28
Children's Outing Association, 39
Christianity, 11, 93-94, 150
Clean Air Act, U.S., 68
clean energy, ii, 35, 67, 72-74
Clean Water Act, U.S., 67
climate change, 23, 58-74, 116,-117, 154
Clinton, William J., President, 118-119
Coke, 28
Coming Good Boom, The, 69
compact living, 29-30, 33, 40-41, 48-49, 56-58, 68-69, 74, 79, 87-88, 129, 165
cooperatives, 140-163

Coors, 161
consciousness, 22, 43, 50, 121-122, 124-125, 128
conservatives, ii, 9, 12, 60-61, 67, 102, 112, 116, 164
consumerism, ii, 25-26, 97, 109
Council of Foreign Relations, 51
creative class, 33-34, 36, 42, 52, 55
creativity, 36, 40, 89, 97, 100, 107-108, 112
crime, 7, 29, 32

D

Darwinian, 94-95, 116-117, 123-127
Dawn of Day, The, 92
death of God, 93-92, 99
deficit, government, 133
democracy, ii, 14, 26, 62, 65, 98, 120, 140-163, 166-167
democracy, economic, 140-163
density, urban, 29, 31, 33, 41, 57, 74, 77-78, 88
Diderot, Denis, 25, 28
Dionysus, 40, 47, 89-90, 92, 97-98, 100
divinities, 111-113
downtown living, 31-42, 46, 77, 81-82, 129, 165
Dutch, *See Netherlands*.
dwelling, idea of, 110-112

E

earth, 1, 3, 27, 58, 65, 89-92, 96-101, 104,108, 110-113, 129, 153, 163
ecological release, 75
economic
    austerity, 8
    crisis, 8, 15, 17-20, 30, 129-139
    democracy, ii, 140-163
    depression, 15, 26, 90, 132-133
    globalization, 146

growth, 7, 56, 60- 61, 141
inequality, 140-163
innovation, 147
materialism, i, 5, 7-8, 20-30
opportunity, 7, 15-20
prosperity, 7, 15-20
recession, 15, 17, 67, 80, 85-86, 130-131, 133, 166-167
security, ii, 7-9, 20
treadmill, 20, 22-23
economics,
    Keynesian, 133, 166-167
    macro-, 129-139
economies of scale, 70
economy,
    artists and the, 36-42
    clean energy and the, 69-74
    climate change and the, 58-74
    consumption and the, 30, 129-139
    development of the, 60
    efficiency and the, 75
    employee ownership and the, 140-163
    employment and the, 129-139
    environmental quality and the, 58-74
    entropy and the, 75-88, 129, 165
    experience and the, 75-88, 129, 134-139
    happiness and the, 22-23
    housing bubble and the, 131-132
    investment and the, 30, 83, 130-136
    macro-, 129-139
    Millennials and the, 15-20
    philosophy and the, ii, 9, 58, 89, 93-94, 108-111
    post-material values and the, ii, 89, 134-139
    productivity and the, 70, 83-84, 134-135, 137-138, 144, 151, 166-167
    stimulating the, 132-133, 135-138
    study of the, i, 103

urban development and the, 29-41, 49
working hours and the, 50-57, 137-139, 165-167
Egypt, 2, 14, 110, 120, 149-160
employee ownership, 140-163
Employee Stock Ownership Plan (ESOP), 162-163
employment, ii, 2, 8, 20, 35, 42, 47, 54, 56, 72-74, 129, 132, 135, 137-138, 141, 143-146, 148, 154, 165
Endangered Species Act, U.S., 67
energy efficiency, 62, 72, 79
entrepreneur, 51, 144-150, 155-156, 158, 160, 163, 166-167
entrepreneurship,
    social, 145, 147-150, 160, 166-167
entropy, 75-88, 129, 165
environmental protection, 9, 12-13, 18-19, 59
Environmental Protection Agency (EPA), 67, 155
environment,
    Millennials and the, 15-20
    philosophy and the, 58-74, 100, 110-113
    politics and the, 58-74
    post-materialism and the, ii, 9, 12-13, 16-19, 30, 41, 58-74, 76, 87, 99-101, 111-112, 120, 126, 137,148-149, 151-152, 154-155, 158, 160, 162, 165
environmentalist, 16, 41, 66, 100
Eroski, 142, 145-146
eternal return of the same, 98-99
Europe, 7-9, 11, 14, 53-56, 62-63, 68, 98, 135, 137-139, 150, 152-155, 159, 161, 165-167
Eurythmy, 1
evolution, 95-96, 110, 116-117, 121-128
existentialism, 1, 42-45, 119
experience,
    arts and, 75-88
    downtown living and, 75-88
    ecological release and, 75-77
    economy and, i-ii, 2-3, 75-88, 164-167
    entropy and, 75-88, 129, 165

motor vehicles and, 75-88
public goods and, ii, 75-88

F

Facebook, 33, 81, 100, 147
fate, 1, 91, 99, 106, 109
Fifth Avenue, New York, 21
Florida, Richard, 33, 36, 42, 52
flow, psychological, 40, 50
for-itself, 43
Fort Collins, Colorado 161-162
fossil fuels, 67-68, 70-73, 159
fourfold, 111
France, 137, 142, 145
freedom, ii, 1, 13-14, 25, 36, 43, 46, 60, 65, 89, 98, 106, 111, 120, 164
freedom of speech, 6
free expression, 12, 60, 105, 137, 141, 149, 151, 155, 164
free spirits, 93-95, 97-100, 109-110, 113
freeways, 30, 80
Freiburg, Germany, 102
Friedrich Nietzsche: A Philosophical Biography, 96
Ford Explorer, 108

G

Gay Science, The, 92
GDP (Gross Domestic Product), 61-63, 65, 130, 134, 136,165
gender equity, 9, 11, 13, 112, 151
General Assembly, Manhattan, New York, 51
Generation X, 15-17
Germany, 102, 137, 161
global warming, 58-74, 116
God, 13, 16, 21, 23, 93-94, 99, 101, 113, 115, 149, 153
Google, 5, 33, 53, 58, 100, 147

Great Depression, 15, 133
Great Recession, 15, 17, 80, 86,130, 133, 166-167
Greeks, 89-92, 99-100
Greek tragedy, 91
Green Bay Packers, 28, 11
greenhouse gases, ii, 3, 41, 61-62, 64-70, 74, 112, 116
Green Party, 9

H

Hadron Collider, 123
happiness research, 22-23, 50, 53-54, 105
health insurance, 54-57
Heidegger, Martin, 43, 99-102, 104, 106-113
herd, the, 94, 97-98
heritage, 106, 112-113
Higgs boson, 123
high tech, 5-6, 27, 51-52, 77
highways, 30, 71
homosexuality, 9-13
Hosny, Sherif, 156-158, 160
Human, All-To-Human, 92
Hurricane Katrina, 61
hydrogen energy, 69-70, 73
hydroponic farming, 155-158

I

inflation, 7, 67, 70, 84, 134, 136
Inglehart, Ronald, 6
in-itself, 43
Intergovernmental Panel on Climate Change (IPCC), 70,
International Social Survey, 59, 64
iPad, 2, 108
iPhone, 27, 79, 81-82
irrigation, 154, 156, 159-160

Islam, 149-150, 155, 157. *See also*, Muslim.

J

Jordan, Kim, 161
justice, 111, 149

K

Kant, Emanuel, 96
KarmSolar, 159-160
Keynes, John Maynard, 133
Koran, 149, 153, 155
Kyoto Protocol, 61-62, 66

L

Lakefront Brewery, 31
Lake Michigan, 32, 101
Lebesch, Jeff, 161
Left Bank, Paris, France, 38
liberals, ii, 9, 12, 14, 16, 18, 19, 60-62, 64-65, 97, 116, 120, 149, 163-164, 166-167
light rail, 32, 35, 73, 87
Lloyd, Richard, 37, 42
Luddite, 109, 112, 120

M

Madison Avenue, New York, 26
Magnificent Mile, Chicago, 21
Mall of America, 21
Marburg University, Germany, 102
mass transit. *See* public transit.
materialism, i-ii, 16, 20-30, 120, 164, 167
meaning of life, 11, 21, 89, 113

Medicaid, 54
Medicare, 54, 158
memes, 95
metaphysics, 92, 100, 101
middle class, 9, 21, 32, 35, 39-40, 44, 48, 60
Middle East, 110, 155, 157
Millennials,
    arts and, 84-88
    beliefs of, 15-20
    downtown living and, 80-82, 84-88, 164
    employee ownership and, 141
    environment and, 16-20
    motor vehicles and, 80-82, 88
    politics and, 15-20
    post-materialism and, 15-20, 80, 82, 84-86, 88, 141, 164
    religion and, 19
    values and, 15-20
    work and, 141, 164
Millers, 161
Milwaukee, Wisconsin, 32, 36, 38-39, 48-49
Milwaukee River, Wisconsin, 32, 39
Mind and Cosmos, 121
Minneapolis-St. Paul, Minnesota, 34, 49
Mondragon Cooperatives Corporation, 142-150, 163
Mondragon, Spain, 142
Montmartre, Paris, France, 38
motor vehicles, 30, 56, 57, 67-71, 73, 78-80, 82, 86, 88, 108, 129, 142
Muslim, 14, 112, 149-151, 153, 155, 157, 160. *See also,* Islam.

N

Nagel, Thomas, 121-128
national debt, 71-72, 74,

nature, 10, 12, 31, 58, 75, 95, 98, 107-114, 118-119, 124, 126, 128, 153, 165
Nausea, 44
Nazism, 106
Neo-Bohemia, 42
neo-bohemia, 37-38
Netherlands, 56
New Age Movement, 11-12
New Belgian Brewing Company, 161-163
New York City, 21, 35, 48, 51, 79
Nietzsche, Friedrich, 47, 89-90, 92-100, 106, 113
Nile River Valley, Egypt, 150, 154, 157, 159
Nitsch, Herbert, 26
North Beach, San Francisco, California, 38
Northface, 28

O

Obama, Barack, President, U.S., 16, 19, 66, 68, 118-119, 132-133
Obamacare, 55, 116, 119, 138
overman, 34, 36, 38, 158

P

Page, Larry, 5, 147
Paris, France, 38, 44-47, 79
Peace Action Center, 39
Philadelphia, Pennsylvania, 49
philosophy,
    climate change and, 58-74
    death and, 90-94, 99
    evolution and, 94-95, 121-128
    existentialist, 42-45, 119
    moral, 5, 121, 94-95, 100, 125-128
    pragmatist, 114-121, 127-128
    post-materialist, 1-14, 89-128, 164-167

    reality and, 92, 99, 108-109, 114-117, 121-128
    reason and, 121-128
    spirituality and , 98-101, 112-114,
    teleology and, 121-128
photovoltaics, 72
Piketty, Thomas, 140, 143
Plato, 96, 98
politics,
    climate change and, 58-74
    environment and, 58-74
    Millennials and, 15-20
    post-materialism and, 13, 48, 58-74, 116, 120
post-materialism,
    climate change and, 58-74
    democracy and, ii, 62, 65, 98, 120, 140-167
    environment and, ii, 9, 12-13, 16-19, 30, 41, 58-74, 76, 87, 99-101, 111-112, 120, 126, 137, 148-149, 151-152, 154-155, 158, 160, 162, 165
    environmental values and, 58-74
    gender equity and, 9, 11, 13, 112, 151
    Green Party and, 9
    homosexuality and, 9, 13
    libertarian values and, 12, 137
    Millennials and, 15-20, 80, 82, 84-86, 88, 141, 164
    pragmatism and, 114-121, 127-128
    politics and, 13, 48, 58-74, 116, 120
    religion and, 11-12, 14, 16, 21, 89, 100-101, 111, 114, 151
    self-direction and, 10
    self-expression and, 6, 9, 12-14, 16, 19, 33, 36, 58, 60, 82, 101, 114, 118, 149, 155, 165
    social innovation and, 147
    social invention and, 152, 158
    social tolerance and, ii, 6, 10, 19, 101
    spirituality and, i, ii, 11-12, 19, 47, 98, 100-101, 112-114, 164
    survival-self-expression values and, 13
    trust and, 9, 13, 16-19, 65-66, 103

universalism and, 10-14, 58, 62, 64-65, 100, 113, 127
work and, ii, 5, 13, 19, 34-37, 40-57, 86, 94, 100-101, 103, 107, 109-110, 114, 131-167
present-at-hand, 102
professionals, 27, 32-40, 46, 48-49, 51-52, 57
profit maximization, 26, 141
public goods, ii, 12, 64, 75-88, 136-137
public transit, 29, 31-31, 41, 57, 69, 74, 77, 79, 80-81, 86-87, 118, 129

R

ready-to-hand, 102, 108
regression analysis, 59
REI (Recreational Equipment Inc.), 25-26
religion, 11-12, 14, 16, 21, 89, 100-101, 111, 114, 151
Rise of the Creative Class, The, 33, 42, 52
rising prices. *See* inflation.
Riverwest, Milwaukee, Wisconsin, 31-32, 38-39, 48-49
Riverwest Artists Association, 39, 49
Riverwest ArtWalk, 39
Riverwest Neighborhood Association, 39
Riverwest Rainbow Alliance, 39
Rocky Mountains, Colorado, 27
Rorty, Richard, 114-121

S

sacred. *See spirituality.*
Sadat, Anwar, President, Egypt, 152
Salvation Army, 93, 126
San Francisco, California, 34, 38, 48, 51, 58
San Luis Peak, Colorado, 23
Sartre, Jean-Paul, 1, 31, 42-49, 119
scale economies, 70
Schaduf Urban Micro Farms, 156-158, 160

secularist, 13-14
Sekem, 151-155, 157, 159-160
Sekem: A Sustainable Community in the Egyptian Desert, 154
self-creation, 24-25, 40, 92-93, 95-96, 119-120
self-direction, 10
self-expression, 6, 9, 12-14, 16, 19, 33, 36, 58, 60, 82, 101, 114, 118, 149, 155, 165
self-overcoming, 92, 96-97, 99, 119
Shell Oil Company, 158
Silent Generation, 15, 164
Silicon Alley, 51
Silicon Valley, 34, 58
sky, 111-113
Skylight Opera, Milwaukee, Wisconsin, 32
social entrepreneurship, 145, 147-150, 155-156, 158, 160, 166-167
social goals, 6, 10, 141, 147
social invention, 152, 158
social tolerance ii, 6, 10, 19, 101
Socrates, 90-91
solar energy, 73, 159
solar-powered irrigation, 159
Sonoran Desert, 24, 7
spirituality, i, ii, 11-12, 19, 47, 98-101, 109, 111-114, 164
Steiner, Rudolph, 150
streetcar suburbs, 29
suburban expats, 32, 34, 39
suburbanization, 21-34, 39-40, 57, 77, 80, 82, 165
survival. i, 13, 75, 94, 126, 144. *See also* economic security.
Sweden, 8
systematizers, 96-97, 100, 117

T

Tea Party, 120
Tech Meetup, 51

technology, 26-27, 51-52, 69, 84-85, 99, 108-110-111, 120, 142, 155, 158
Third Ward, Milwaukee, Wisconsin, 32, 39
Thus Spoke Zarathustra, 95, 97, 99
tolerance. *See social tolerance.*
Toyota Prius C, 25
Toyota RAV4, 24
tradition, 10-14, 16, 19, 45-47, 51, 86, 93-94, 100, 106-107, 112-114, 149, 156, 160
trust, 9, 13, 16-19, 65
Twitchell, James, 23-24, 26-28

U

unemployment, 8, 22, 30, 37, 56, 74, 130, 133-135, 139, 166-167
unions, 9, 40, 84
United Nations Environmental Program (UNEP), 141-142
universalism, 10-14, 58, 62, 64-65, 100, 113, 127
University of London, 158
University of Michigan, 6
University of Wisconsin-Milwaukee (UWM), 32
urban development,
    and artists, 31, 36-40, 46, 48-49, 55-57, 86
    and density, 29, 31, 33, 41, 57, 74, 77-78, 88
urban living, 31, 33, 42, 57, 77, 79, 165
U.S. (United States), 8, 12, 14, 18-20, 30, 53-56, 61-62, 66-68, 71, 73, 129-130, 132, 135-138, 148, 161, 163

V

values,
    environmental, 58-74
    libertarian, 12, 137
    materialist, i-ii, 16, 20-30, 120, 164, 167
    Millennials and, 15-20
    post-materialist, 1-20, 42-49, 58-128, 164-167

    pragmatic, 114-121, 127-128
    survival-self-expression, 13
    traditional-secular/rational, 13-14
    universalist, 10-14, 58, 62, 64-65, 100, 113, 127
Van Gogh, Vincent, 118
virtues, 27, 89, 97

W

Wicker Park, Chicago, Illinois, 37-39, 42-50
willingness-to-pay, 59-60, 62
Will to Power, Attempt at Revaluation of All Values, 96
will to power, 95-97
wind energy, 69-73, 162
work, ii, 5, 13, 19, 34-57, 132-147, 153, 160-167
working hours, ii, 50-57, 165-167
World Values Survey, 13, 20, 59, 63
World War I, 102
World War II, 29-30, 80

Y

Yon Kippur War, 67
Young, Julian, 96

Z

Zahran, Ahmed, 158-160
Zamalek, Cairo, Egypt, 157
Zarathustra, 95, 97-99
Zygna, 52

www.ingramcontent.com/pod-product-compliance
Lightning Source LLC
Chambersburg PA
CBHW051647170526
45167CB00001B/364